15.95

Dominic Savio
Teenage Saint

Peter Lappin

Post Office Box 2286, Fort Collins, CO 80522

IMPRIMI POTEST:
JAMES SZAFORZ, S.D.B.
CENSOR DEPUTATUS

NIHIL OBSTAT:
JOHN A. SCHULIEN, S.T.D.
CENSOR LIBRORUM

IMPRIMATUR:
ALBERTUS G. MEYER
ARCHIEPISCOPUS MILWAUCHIENSIS

JULY 7, 1954

ISBN 0-912141-97-2

CONTENTS

To
the teenage saint that lies
hidden away in the heart
of every boy and girl

Dominic Savio
Teenage Saint

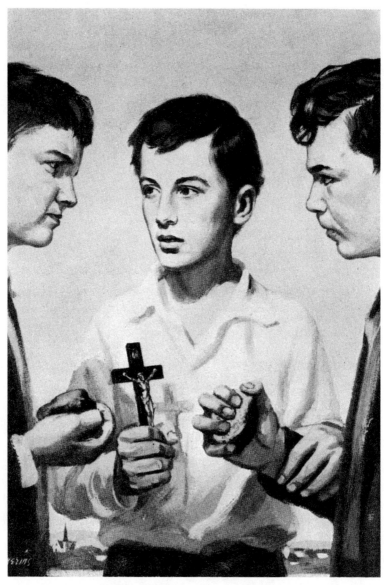

"Here's the condition: You've got to throw
the first stone at me!" (Page 71.)

CHAPTER 1

SPARKS FROM THE FORGE

CHARLES SAVIO washed his hands at the rain barrel outside the smithy and looked up at the sky. It was a lovely summer evening in the little village of Murialdo in the north of Italy, and he could see the Alps darkening against the white clouds. He went inside the smithy again and wiped his hands dry on an old stained cloth that hung on a nail beside the door. The smithy fire was dying and he banked it up with gray-and-black ashes so that it would smolder all night and be ready for the next day. He slammed the door of the smithy, shot home the bolt, and snapped shut the heavy padlock. Digging his hands deep into his pockets contentedly, he set off for his home on the outskirts of the village.

Charles was not yet thirty. Of medium build, he was noticeably slight for a blacksmith. When he smiled, two remarkably blue eyes twinkled and lit up his whole face. Quiet and humble in his ways, he was not a man to haggle over prices at the smithy. He never had to. One

1

look at his face and somehow even the strangers knew his price was fair.

His wife Bridgit sometimes lost patience with him, especially when she thought he should have insisted more on his rights. She always stood up for hers. Yet even she could never put much heart into the scolding. She was too well aware that her husband could not help being as good-natured with the customers at the smithy as he was with his family at home.

This evening Charles' mind was filled with pleasant thoughts. He was thinking of home, his wife and children, of his good warm supper, and of his easy chair. Maybe later he'd go to the choir. He sang baritone, and the neighbors often told him how they liked his voice.

He raised his head as he came toward the house, and saw a small figure standing in the doorway. The figure waved its hands and came running toward him. With a sweep of his strong arms, Charles caught up the five-year-old boy and raised him high in the air.

Charles was fond of his son Dominic. Born in Riva di Chieri, about five miles west of Murialdo, he had come to help his parents forget their sorrow after their first boy died when only two weeks old. Dominic, also, had looked so frail and puny on the morning of his birth, April 2, 1842, that his father had rushed him that same evening to the parish church for baptism.

"Ooooh, my little Dominic! Did you take care of Mamma and mind the house while Daddy was away?"

"Yes, Daddy, but I'm not tired and you are. Do I make you tired, Daddy?"

"*You* make me tired? Why, you make me the happiest

man in the whole world, and I wouldn't sell you for all the gold in a pirate's treasure chest!"

Dominic climbed upon his father's back, put his legs over his shoulders, and leaned forward so that his father's large horny hands could hold his own tiny ones securely.

"Dominic," said his father after a few steps.

"Yes, Daddy?" Dominic's voice jumped in his throat as he was jogged along on his father's shoulders.

"I have something in my pocket."

"What?"

"Guess."

"Fruit?"

"No."

"Candy?"

"No."

"Come on, Daddy! Tell me what!"

"I have four shining new pennies for the one who loves me best of all."

Dominic put his arms around his father's neck and pulled tight. The cords stood out blue-black on the other's sunburned skin. Then he kissed his father's rough, unshaven cheek and felt the stiff hairs press into his own soft skin.

"There!" said Dominic. "Don't I love you best?"

"Yes; but you wouldn't want to choke me, would you?"

"Do I get the pennies?"

"I suppose you do. But tell me, son, what did you do with the other pennies I gave you?"

"Oh Daddy! Some poor people came and Mommy didn't have anything to give them. She said she gave to a lot of them already. They went away so sad, and

I nearly cried. So I ran after them and gave them all my pennies."

"What will you do with these new pennies?"

"I don't know, Daddy." There was a slight pause in the conversation. Then Dominic asked: "Are you angry with me?"

"Yes, I'm so angry with you I could eat you up!"

Charles swung Dominic down into his arms, buried his rugged face in the little bundle the boy made, and snarled in imitation of a lion devouring its prey.

They were both laughing when they stopped before a small, two-story house, with an outside stairway to the second floor. The house was very old and not too well built, but it had recently been repaired and whitewashed. They entered the kitchen-living room which had an uneven earthen floor. Two doors led from the kitchen into adjacent bedrooms. The furniture was poor, but everything was in its proper place and the house had an air of neatness and comfort about it.

Bridgit Savio was leaning over the wide hearth stirring a large black pot suspended from a hook. Yellow and red flames danced around the bottom of the pot. There was a milky smell in the air from the boiling polenta. In the center of the kitchen a table was set for four.

Bridgit turned to the new arrivals. She was about the same height as Charles. Her hair was brushed smooth over her head and down her neck. She wore a blue apron over a dress of faded gray that was so long it fell over her slippered feet. Bridgit did not smile much. She had to work hard both inside and outside the home to keep her growing family clothed and fed. But she succeeded in managing things so well, even in those difficult times, that the neighbors marveled how she did it and often said so, to Bridgit's great satisfaction.

"Mamma," Charles called out, "here's two hungry men who want food!"

"That young fellow can wait a while," said Bridgit, dryly, nodding toward Dominic. "He's just had his. What's more, you're going to have to talk to that son of yours."

"Oh?" said Charles in surprise. "What did he do?"

Dominic, still holding his father's hand, stepped back a little and stared at the floor.

"You know how hard it is to find enough to put on the table these days," said Bridgit.

"Yes, I know, dear. So?"

"Well, an hour or so ago, I gave him a piece of white bread and a slice of polenta. What did he do but walk out of the house, and the next thing I see, he's giving it to some stranger on his way to Chieri."

"And I saw him giving some money to a man at the door," chimed in a voice from one of the nearby bedrooms. A little girl came out and ran to greet her father.

This was Raimonda, Dominic's younger sister. She was dark and pretty and had a lovely smile. Dominic was very fond of Raimonda, but there were times when her girl's tricks made him mad. This was one of the times.

Dominic took a step toward her and she backed away quickly.

"It was my own money," he said hotly. "And you're just a tattletale, that's what *you* are. Do I tell stories on you?"

"That's enough, you two," Bridgit warned.

"She's always telling tales," protested Dominic, in tears. "If I just hit her the way other boys hit their sisters, I guess she wouldn't talk so much."

Raimonda did not say another word. She just kept her eyes fixed on her brother.

Charles turned to Dominic and braced himself. He was not fitted for this kind of task.

"Now look here, Dominic," he began. "Remember that food costs a lot of money these days, and you just can't go on giving things away. Do you hear?" He caught the look in Dominic's upturned eyes and finished lamely, "Now let's sit down to supper and have no more of this nonsense!"

When the meal was finished, Charles pushed his chair back and went over to the fire. Bridgit, assisted by Raimonda, began to clear away the supper things from the table. From across the valley, where the tiny church of Murialdo clung to the side of a vine-covered hill, came the chimes of the evening bell. The sound of the bell seemed to hush for a moment everything else in the house; but only for a moment. Bridgit went on with her chores, and Charles settled more comfortably into his chair by the fire for an after-supper nap.

"Mommy," Dominic said softly.

"What is it, dear?"

"That's the Angelus, Mommy."

There was a moment's silence. Then Bridgit spoke.

"Listen, my fine young man," she said, looking down at him. "If you think your own mother doesn't know her duties just because she hasn't the time to hide away somewhere and spend a couple of hours on her knees like you, you're very much mistaken. No one has to tell me what to do. Charles, wake up! That's the Angelus."

Charles struggled wearily to his feet.

"The Angel of the Lord declared unto Mary . . ." Bridgit began, as she wiped her glistening hands in her apron.

"Mommy, it's so late! You promised you'd wake me up!" Dominic looked as if he were going to cry.

"So I did, dear," said Bridgit, "but it looks so bad outside. It's freezing, darling, and I was sure you wouldn't want to go out on a morning like this."

"But I have to serve Mass! Father John says I'm big enough to serve alone now, and this very morning he was going to let me serve all by myself!"

"All right, dear. There's still time. The bell hasn't rung, so Father John can't have come yet. I wouldn't blame him if he didn't turn up in weather like this."

Dominic rose to wash and dress. He saw the snow reaching up high along the sides of the windows. Outside everything was muffled and strangely quiet. After a quick breakfast of soup and bread he pulled on his woolen cap and wound a long muffler round his neck.

"Mind you, don't stand out in the cold!" Bridgit called after him as he slammed the door firmly behind him to keep out the biting wind. Dominic pulled his cap so far down over his forehead and ears that he looked like a gnome. With only a pair of eyes blinking from between several layers of muffler and his hands dug deep into his pockets, he chomped with his wooden shoes through the snow and ice down the road to Mass.

The night's heavy snowfall lay white and unbroken about the church. The priest had not yet arrived and the door of the church was still locked. Murialdo was not big enough to have a resident pastor, and Father John from nearby Mondonio served as chaplain. Dominic snuggled into a corner of the high doorway and settled down on his heels to wait.

Before long a dark figure approached, etched sharply against the white background of snow. It had a thick mantle swathed about its head and shoulders. The figure moved along soundlessly, as quickly as the swirling folds of cassock and cape would allow. Behind it stretched two long parallel lines of deep, gray footprints.

"Bless my soul! Is it you, Dominic?" exclaimed the priest in surprise, when he saw the boy curled up in the doorway.

Dominic watched the way the priest's breath made smoke as he talked. He himself did not speak, but smiled and waited until the priest had opened the door. Then he rose and followed him.

While Father John, with Dominic's help, prepared the vestments, he thought he would have some fun with the boy. Dominic's answers were so straightforward and naïve they often made him laugh. As he drew out a long shallow drawer in which the vestments were laid out, he looked at Dominic.

"Dominic," he said, shaking his head in doubt, "somehow I think you're rather on the small side to be serving Mass alone."

"Oh, but I know all the words, Father! And I've done

all the rest lots of times with the other boys . . . and lots of times by myself."

"Do you say Mass at home, Dominic?"

"Well, you know, Father . . . just play-acting. . . ."

"Yes, but how about your height, Dominic? You're too small for the Missal. Why, you're not even as high as the altar!"

"I know, Father . . . but maybe you could help me. You know . . ."

"All right, Dominic. If you get into any difficulty with the Missal, just call for help."

"Oh Father, I don't need to *call* for help. That would disturb the Mass. Just pull the bookstand over to the edge of the altar so I can reach it, that's all. You don't have to worry, Father. I'll get by."

"All right, then. Let's go. But the Lord help you if you drop any Latin words on my feet!"

"Introibo ad altare Dei. . . . I will go in to the altar of God. To God, Who giveth joy to my youth."

Father John glanced at the tumbling blond hair of the boy at his side, and smiled. Then he brushed away the distraction and gave his whole attention to the Mass.

When the difficult responses were over, Dominic began to wonder about the angels who were supposed to surround the altar during Mass. He'd never seen any. Did they ever sit down? Did their breath smoke in the cold? Did they . . .

"Deo gratias!" He quickly answered the priest's glance in his direction, and moved to the epistle side. This was for him the most anxious moment of the Mass. He liked to serve Mass, but he hated having to shift that heavy book. It was set away back on the altar; it was so big it covered his chest, and so weighty it made him top-heavy. When he walked across the altar steps it nearly toppled him over.

Father John saw two blue eyes signal to him and under-stood. He drew the bookstand as near to the edge of the altar table as it was safe to do. Dominic stood on his tiptoes. The fingers of his outstretched arms groped for, and found, the bottom of the stand; he tipped the stand up so that the edge rested against his chin. From there he slipped it down to his chest. He was all set. He climbed down the steps carefully, feeling his way. At the bottom he crossed over to the other side. He felt with his foot for the bottom step, climbed it. He felt for the second, climbed it. He felt for the third, raised his foot . . . suddenly the book shifted on the stand, pushed him back, pulled him forward. . . . Down crashed book and bookstand with Dominic underneath!

Dominic got up quickly, however, snapped the book-stand rest into the proper slant, put the Missal on it, and placed both on the altar. Then he flipped the Missal open at the red marker and made his way down again to the bottom of the steps.

"At that time, Jesus said to his disciples: Unless ye become as little children . . ."

Father John signed himself with his thumb, glanced out of the corner of his eye, and saw a small white face with red lips set in a grim little smile.

One afternoon Charles Savio told his wife that a

friend, who was coming up to talk about a piece of work at the smithy, would stay for supper. It meant no trouble for Bridgit, for the meals of the Savios were not complicated. She prepared some extra polenta and laid out a bowl, glass, knife, and spoon opposite an extra chair. A white cloth was spread on the table in deference to the "company."

At suppertime Big Joe Bianchi arrived with Charles. "Hello, Bridgit! How are you, children?" he boomed. He prided himself on his bluff ways.

"So that's the little fellow you were telling me about down at the forge?" he said to Charles. " 'Little Angel' eh?" Then to Dominic — "And have you started to grow your wings yet to fly to heaven?" The remark was accompanied by a laugh, neither sarcastic nor full of humor. "Goin' to take a mighty big pair of wings to carry *me* to heaven, eh Charley? Ho, ho, ho!"

He seated himself at the table, took up the potbellied canteen of red wine, and poured himself a glassful. He held up the glass, looked through it, then threw back his head and drained it.

"Heh!" he gasped, wiping his mouth with the back of his hand. He took up the spoon and rubbed it clean with his thumb. Carving himself a large spoonful from his portion of polenta, he pushed it into his mouth. It was too hot. He began to suck in air noisily to cool the hot mouthful.

"Aah! Ooooh! Aaah!" he panted, his eyes darting wildly around the room.

It was some time before Big Joe noticed that Dominic was no longer opposite him at the table.

"Oh," he said, when his mouth had cooled enough to allow him to speak, "young one gone?"

Charles and Bridgit said nothing, but Bridgit gave a sidelong glance at Charles and blushed. Charles quickly drew the conversation round to the smithy.

Soon the frugal meal was finished. Big Joe rose to go. Charles accompanied him to the door. When his friend had gone, Charles went over to Dominic who was sitting in a corner with his bowl between his knees.

"Why did you get up from the table like that?" he asked.

"Well, Daddy," answered the boy quietly, "I didn't want to stay beside anyone who sits down to eat like an animal, without first saying grace."

Charles started to say a sharp word about good manners, but as he looked at Dominic something seemed to occur to him, and he left the words unsaid. For a five-year-old, Dominic often did and said things that surprised him. They weren't wrong, of course. It was just that you didn't expect them from a child so young.

CHAPTER 2

DEATH BEFORE SIN!

"WHERE'S Dominic?"

"Oh, he's in church, praying. He wants to be a saint!"

This was the only thing the other boys thought strange about Dominic when, at the age of six, he was enrolled in the elementary classes of Father John's village school at Murialdo. And if Dominic had been able to find a more out-of-the-way place for his praying, they would not have noticed even that. He never made a demonstration of his religion. Neither was he ever ashamed to show it.

It did not take the alert Father John long to become aware that there was something out of the ordinary about Dominic. He had often seen him come with his mother to church. He remembered how Dominic used to wait for him, hail, rain, or snow, and kneel down on the cold, wet ground until he opened the church. If they met on the street, the boy would always say politely, "Good morning, Father!" and walk a little way with him. He had heard the other boys invite him to go along with them on their usual escapades — throwing stones, breaking into orchards, or making fun of old people — but Dominic had always refused. He had continued to refuse even when the bigger boys threatened to punch his nose for not going. The priest remembered also Dominic's mortal terror of the heavy Mass book and he smiled every time he thought of it falling down the altar steps and pulling Dominic down along with it.

"He is a child of great promise," he exclaimed one day to his friends. "God grant that such a promise may be fulfilled!"

The great Napoleon used to say that the happiest day of his life was the day of his First Communion. Yet his First Communion and that of Dominic Savio had hanging over both of them the shadow of a heresy called Jansenism.

Jansenists taught that Catholics should receive Holy Communion only after long and serious preparation, at the most only once or twice a year, and then with great fear and trembling. As for children of Dominic's age — not by any means!

Father John was not a Jansenist, but he did not like just yet to make an open stand against the current practice. When Dominic, therefore, at the age of seven, begged to be allowed to receive his First Communion with that year's group, Father John hesitated.

"I'll have to think this over," he said. He decided first to consult Father Cugliero, an old classmate from seminary days.

"Look, Father," he told his friend, "when that boy was

only five years old, if he found the church door closed early in the morning, he would kneel down right there and wait until it opened. The weather never worried him. He'd kneel down in mud as soon as on dry ground. I tell you I found him outside the church one winter morning waiting to serve my Mass, and he was actually stiff with the cold!"

When Father Cugliero heard the other's description of Dominic's conduct, he decided immediately: if the boy can distinguish between bread and the Eucharist, let him receive.

"Now that we have agreed," said Father Cugliero, "that as far as *he* is concerned, he should be allowed to make his First Communion, there's still another difficulty."

"What's that?"

"How will the parents of the other boys take it? They are sure to complain at such a preference."

"No," said Father John. "I don't think so. They all look upon Dominic as an exceptionally good boy. I'm sure they will not feel offended."

"What will the other parents say?" This was the only objection several other priests could find against allowing Dominic to receive his First Communion at such an early age. The two priests, therefore, boldly decided to violate the custom still in use of not permitting children to receive until they had reached the age of eleven or twelve. When Father John returned to Murialdo he told Dominic to go ahead and prepare to make his First Communion.

Dominic was delighted, and on the eve of what he ever afterward called "the great day" he went to his mother. It was the custom in those parts for children to approach their parents on the eve of First Communion, and ask forgiveness for anything they might have done to give offense. The parents were then supposed to tell the children what faults they should be careful to correct.

The only words Dominic's mother could find for the occasion were: "Darling, I hope God always keeps you good!"

"Do you forgive me, Mommy, for everything I've done?"

"Of course, son." Burying the memory of the thousand and one moments when he had unwittingly annoyed and vexed her in a warm embrace, his mother said: "Pray that Mommy and Daddy may be very good."

"Oh, no," said Dominic earnestly. "I think you're good enough already!" That was worth another hug.

John Cagliero, one of the boys who received Communion with Dominic on Easter Sunday, 1849, says that the congregation stared at the boy as he approached the altar rail. This was the first time people noticed the air of modesty that later was to become so characteristic of him.

As to what Dominic felt when he first received Holy Communion, we can only guess. He always referred to that day with delight. "I did not know," he declared, "whether I was in heaven or on earth!"

For the occasion, he made four resolutions:

1. He would sanctify the Sundays and holydays.
2. His friends would be Jesus and Mary.
3. He would go to Confession more often, and to Holy Communion as often as allowed.
4. *He would prefer death rather than sin!*

Someone has said that this last resolution sounds too forceful to come from one who, after all, was only seven years old. But Dominic was always described as being rather ahead of his years, especially in what concerned the knowledge and practice of his Faith. Though not a genius, he was, throughout his schooling, among the four leading members of his class.

This resolution, "Death before sin," places him side by side with the little saint of our own time, St. Maria Goretti, the martyr of purity. Their similarity lies in the firm intention both had of giving their lives before they would offend God by committing sin. Maria Goretti, however, was offered the opportunity to lay down her life to prove her intention. Dominic was not. Apparently God did not want a schoolboy martyr as a model. The death offered to Dominic was the death of his flesh, a slow martyrdom of mortification and penance that he accepted with a characteristic little smile on his lips — a martyrdom that was later illustrated in a vision Don Bosco had of Dominic shortly after the boy's death.

Dominic was seven years old when he took this first important step along the road to sanctity.

CHAPTER 3

ADVENTURES ALONG THE WAY

DURING Dominic's early school days, Father John noticed something else about his pupil: Dominic was not fond of quarreling. He always backed out of the fights so frequent among his friends. The reason for this, he explained later to Don Bosco, was not because he was afraid but because he felt hurt when he saw anyone else suffer. Once the sight of two boys being slapped by the teacher caused him so much pain that he burst into tears. "I'd rather the teacher would beat me," he confessed, "than watch him beat one of the others."

Not that Dominic did not have a temper of his own. He had a very quick temper which he had to fight against to keep under control. And he was not always too successful in this during those early days. A boy named Vaschetti (later Monsignor Vaschetti) had a quarrel with him. Dominic lost his temper and punched him. Until his death, Monsignor Vaschetti was proud to show inquirers exactly how Dominic Savio had punched his head!

"I should like to record that he once attacked me in a sudden burst of temper," Monsignor Vaschetti said. "He was quick-tempered, sometimes even violent. He held stubbornly to his own opinions. Afterward, however, he would always feel sorry for it."

By this time, Dominic had outgrown the little village school at Murialdo, and his parents faced the problem of providing for his further education. Had the Savios been better off when he finished his elementary grades, he would have had little difficulty in continuing his studies at a boarding school. But since they were poor, Dominic had to choose between giving up his studies altogether, or walking several miles each day to attend a higher grade school at Castelnuovo. There was, of course, the possibility that his parents would refuse to let him carry on his studies. They might hire him out to a farm, or start him out, instead, in some trade where he could bring home a little extra help. They sorely needed help in those days.

Dominic himself, however, insisted that he should continue to study. "I've got to go to school," he kept repeating. "If I'm to become a priest, I've got to go to school."

From this moment on Dominic somehow began to give the impression to those around him that within him there was some kind of force which kept spurring him on as if according to some definite plan. When he expressed a wish to do something, he would never say simply, "I should like to," or "If only I could." He always said instead, "I want to," or "I must!"

This urgency is one of the curious features of Dominic's

life. Divine Providence seems to have marked him out early for a definite purpose, and he seemed somehow to understand it and to act accordingly.

He did not take long to form a clear idea of what he wanted and nothing, he once declared, was going to stop him from getting it. Teenagers by the thousands, even from their earliest years, know what they want and are determined to get it. But they usually have very temporal ambitions. What Dominic wanted was to become a saint.

"I want to become a saint," he declared. "And if I don't become one, I'm a failure."

These are the words he repeated most emphatically to Don Bosco when he was confronted with the question that older people always ask: "And what are *you* going to be, my little man?"

Dominic's determination showed itself frequently during his early life — with the man who forgot to say grace, for instance; with the boys of the village who beat him for not doing something against his conscience. Now it reappeared in his desire to carry on his studies.

After much coaxing, the Savios agreed to let Dominic study at Castelnuovo. He was received into the school, by coincidence, on June 21, the Feast of St. Aloysius Gonzaga, 1851, by Father Alexander Allora.

Obtaining the necessary permission from his parents, however, was only half the battle. The other half was the three mile trip to and from Castelnuovo which had to be made twice around every day. It was a long way and Dominic had to walk. In winter the bitter cold brought agony to his bare hands and badly-shod feet. He soon learned the value of chilblains and cold sores as a source of mortification. In hot weather the blazing sun beat down on him without mercy, for the road was high and without shade. Moreover, it was a road infested with bandits. Don Bosco told Dominic how he had been held up by a bandit on that very road. Fortunately, he had recognized the man as a fallen-away acquaintance. He ended up by persuading the bandit to kneel down and make a good confession!

One summer morning Dominic set off as usual for the school at Castelnuovo. Although it was already summer, the schools had not yet closed in the city. Unlike the country people, the town dwellers felt no need of closing school early to let the children stay home to help with the crops.

The sun was still low in the morning sky, but already puffs of warm air played about his bare feet and legs and gave promise of another scorching day. Long before he was within sight of Castelnuovo the perspiration was already rolling down his face. All at once he heard someone hail him. "Savio! Savio!"

He looked around and saw four others from his class coming up behind him. Each of them, like himself, had a small bundle of books under his arm.

"Phew!" said Fanti, the biggest boy, and the one generally accepted as the leader of the class. "You walk all the way?"

"Have to," said Dominic. "There's nobody to carry me."

Fanti was not sure if the laugh that followed was

aimed at him, but after giving the matter a moment's thought in his dull mind, he dropped it. He turned his attention to something more important.

"School's closing soon," he said to nobody in particular.

"Yes," said one of the boys. "Won't be long now till exams and then — whoopee!"

"Not much to do before exams," said Fanti.

"No," said another. "Just stick around. Teacher doesn't bother much."

"We might as well not be there at all," said the third boy.

Fanti stopped dead.

"Say!" he said. "That's an idea! We might just as well not be there. That's right. Suppose we weren't there? Suppose we took a rest? Guess we need it after all the studying we've done. How about it, fellas?"

"I'm game," said one.

"So'm I," said another.

"Me, too," said the third.

That left only Dominic.

"Whadya say, Savio?" asked Fanti. "You coming?"

Dominic did not say anything. He had not made up his mind. School certainly wasn't much of a pleasure on a sweltering day like this. He'd be so tired when he got there he'd be sure to fall asleep. He'd done so yesterday and the day before. Besides, there weren't really any classes. . . .

"Snap out of it, Savio! Make up your mind. What harm is there anyway in taking one day off?"

"All right," said Dominic. "I'll come."

A short distance ahead the five boys left the road and

cut along a path that led to the woods. They started planning as they went how they would spend that wonderful day of freedom. They walked for about fifteen minutes. Then Dominic stopped.

"Fanti," he said. "I don't feel right."

"How come?" said Fanti. "You sick?"

"No," said Dominic. "It's just that I don't feel I'm doing right."

"Say, what's the matter with you, anyway? Turning sissy?" asked Fanti impatiently.

"I think I'll go back," said Dominic. "If I went on with you, I wouldn't enjoy myself, so I might as well go back."

He turned and walked back in the direction they had come from. The others jeered and catcalled after him, but he kept on until he reached school, and settled down to the morning's classwork as if nothing out of the ordinary had happened.

Perhaps attending school at Castelnuovo really was a little too much for Dominic. If it was not too much for his determination, it undoubtedly was for his frail young body. His health began to show signs of strain and his parents began to worry. Others, too, began to criticize. The neighbors who passed their spare time at night gossiping in the warmth of the cow barns had plenty to say about Bridgit Savio. Bridgit Savio, they said, should know better than to let her son, who wasn't exactly a mule for strength, mind you, travel those dangerous roads alone, school or no school. One of them said she'd ask Robert Negri, whose farm lay alongside Dominic's route, to talk to the child. Robert could point out that Dominic shouldn't be making the trip every day. Dominic would tell his mother and then, if Bridgit had any sense at all, she'd take the hint.

Robert agreed, and one afternoon he lay in wait for Dominic. While he was waiting, he pretended to be busy.

It was not long before the figure of the boy appeared at the bend of the road that marked off Robert's land. Robert braced himself for the meeting.

"Hey, lad!" he called out as the boy came closer.

"Afternoon, Signor Negri," said Dominic.

Robert dropped stiffly onto the road from the ridge that served as a hedge.

"You do a lot of walking, Dominic," said Robert. "Don't you ever feel tired?"

"Guess I do feel very tired sometimes."

"And, say, aren't you scared to travel along roads like these alone?"

"I suppose I would be scared, Signor Negri, if I had to travel alone. But I don't travel alone."

"Not alone? How come?"

"Well, I have my Guardian Angel with me and we talk over things together. Besides it isn't so bad when you work for someone who pays you well."

"You mean someone pays you for this?"

"That's right, Signor Negri."

"Who?"

"Our Blessed Lord."

"Ooooh, I see! — Well, good luck, son."

"Good-by, Signor Negri."

Robert watched the boy continue his journey down the road. He pushed his hat back on his head. "Talks things over with his Guardian Angel, heh? — Someone who pays him well. My, oh my!" he exclaimed to himself as he climbed over the ridge again into his own land.

Now he could read some sense into what he had seen a couple of days before. He had watched two or three youngsters around a barn dance, trying to push Dominic into the middle of the dancers. He remembered they had been jibing at the boy. "Let's see the little priest dance a step or two," they said. The boy, however, had blushed and left them.

Dominic had spoken with conviction of his Guardian Angel. There seemed to exist between the two an unusual degree of familiarity. Other incidents illustrate how large a part his Guardian Angel played in Dominic's life.

One evening, said Dominic's father, Dominic and he were returning from a *festa* in a neighboring town in honor of the local saint. It had been glorious weather and the fun and excitement had kept them constantly on the move. On the way back it was about as much as Dominic could do to drag his feet along the ground.

Suddenly a young man appeared at Dominic's side. Without a word, he took the tired boy into his arms and carried him the rest of the journey. Dominic slept the whole way home. When they reached the house the young man put Dominic, still only half awake, down at the door and disappeared. To the end of his days, Dominic's father maintained that from the way the young man suddenly appeared from nowhere and just as suddenly disappeared, he must have been an angel.

Not long after this another incident occurred that set people wondering.

Dominic and Raimonda were one day playing near the river's edge. Dominic left his sister to chase the frogs that were sunning themselves like old men on the bank. The frogs grunted with displeasure when they saw him and plopped into the water out of sight. Then all was silent again, except for the bubbling of the river as it raced past Dominic's feet.

Suddenly a scream rang out.

"Help! Help!"

Then there was a loud splash.

Raimonda had fallen in!

With all her clothing on, she was in danger of drowning quickly in the swift current.

Dominic immediately ran to her rescue and somehow dragged her, wet clothes and all, out of the river and up the bank to safety.

When the children reached home and their parents had recovered from the shock, they began to inquire how it had happened. They talked about how tragic it might have been for both Dominic and his sister. It was only then that they realized just what a feat it must have been on Dominic's part to drag his sister from the river. They showed surprise at his strength.

"Oh, no," said Dominic frankly. "It wasn't just *my* strength. While I was pulling at one of her arms, my Guardian Angel came to help me and he pulled at the other arm!"

Years later, when he had to leave Don Bosco's Oratory for a while and come home for a rest, he arrived at Castelnuovo after a long, tiring journey from Turin. There he found that no one had come to meet him. His letter

The house where Dominic was born, on the
outskirts of Riva di Chieri.

The chapel and walled-in cemetery where
Dominic was buried the first time.

Above: Municipal building, church and tower, Riva di Chieri.

Right: Scene of Dominic's baptism, with commemorative plaque.

advising his parents that he was coming home had not yet reached them. He had to walk the rest of the way to Moriondo, and carry his luggage as well. By the time he reached the house he was exhausted.

"My poor child!" exclaimed his mother when she saw him. "Did you have to come all the way from Castelnuovo alone?"

"No, Mother," replied Dominic. "When I got down from the coach there was a beautiful Lady who was kind enough to accompany me and help me with my bag."

"Why didn't you invite her in at least to rest a while?"

"I couldn't, Mother. As soon as we reached the village, she disappeared."

CHAPTER 4

HERO OR HYPOCRITE?

IT IS not certain why the Savios moved again. Probably it was still because of their need to earn enough to take care of their ever growing family. In October, 1852, they moved from Murialdo back to Mondonio. Charles Savio had lived here before he married.

The change was a welcome one for Dominic. His marks for the first four months at Castelnuovo were registered as "excellent." Father Alexander said his success was not due to any brilliance on his part, but rather to his constancy in applying himself to the work he had in hand. At the end of his session at the school in Castelnuovo, however, he fell sick, though not seriously, and had to go to bed for a while to rest. His parents then transferred him from the Castelnuovo school with its killing twelve mile walk each day, to the school at Mondonio. This had the higher grades that Dominic now needed. Father John Cugliero was in charge.

Dominic was delighted to find some of his old friends

28

in school at Mondonio. They, too, had come up from Murialdo for the higher grades. Among these was Angelo Savio. Angelo was a friend but no relation. It was to Angelo, about this time, that he mentioned his desire to become a priest.

"Angelo," he said one day as they were walking home from school together, "I want to become a priest."

"What do you want to do that for?"

"I want to be able to save souls."

"Has your dad any money?"

"If he has, nobody ever saw it."

"Then you might as well hope to fly as hope to be a priest," Angelo concluded sagely. "It takes an awful lot of money."

It was a difficulty Dominic had never thought existed. He wondered to himself how it would ever be overcome.

One morning Dominic came to school early. He had plenty to do before the class began, for as a new boy it was his duty to clean out the stove and reset it, ready for the teacher to light according to his custom. It was a dismal task, working with that cold and dusty stove. No matter how softly he raked out the ashes, clouds of gray dust would rise and catch the back of the nostrils with an acrid taste.

By the time the stove was cleaned and ready for a fresh fire, most of the boys had arrived and were having fun at the back of the classroom. Very soon they split up into opposing camps and engaged in a noisy battle. The main ammunition was wet paper balls.

The boys obligingly held their fire when Dominic went

out for the day's supply of wood. When he reappeared, his arms full of sticks, the battle had subsided.

Dominic set the fire, making good use of some of the paper he recovered from the floor. He laid down the light, dry kindling, and on top of that the heavier wood for burning. When it was set, he felt like putting a match to it to see the final success of his handiwork. That, however, was not part of his chore. The stove had to be set and left set until the teacher arrived. The teacher himself would apply the match.

When all was ready, Dominic, with a final sweep around the iron base of the stove, came away and sat down to prepare himself for class. A period of moderate silence prevailed.

"Say!" exclaimed one of the boys suddenly. "Know what?"

"No," said the others.

"Let's fix the stove!"

"But it's already fixed. Savio fixed it."

"Yeah, but not the way I mean," said the first. He rose, went outside, and returned with his arms full of large round stones. He dropped them heavily on the floor. Then he lifted the lid from the stove, took out the biggest sticks, and to the surprise of the others, put the stones in their place. He closed the stove, put the extra wood on the pile, and came back to his desk. All comments were cut short by the opening of the door.

"Good morning, Father!"

"Morning, boys!"

Father Cugliero unwound the folds of his large, black cape and immediately gave his attention to the stove.

Rubbing his dry palms noisily together, he bent down and opened the little iron door. He was so used to the routine he did not even look to see if the fire had been laid. Instead, he applied a lighted match to the paper in one or two places, waited until the paper was well lit, then threw the match into the heart of the flames and banged the iron door shut.

He looked up sharply. Had he heard something — a giggle? He must have been mistaken. Every head was bent over a book and lips were moving in urgent, whispered preparation.

Turning to the textbooks on his desk he took up the one on top, opened it at a marker, and with his back as close as was convenient to the fast-warming stove, commenced the morning session. As question and answer continued, he began to sense rather than feel that things were not quite what they should be. He was inclined at first to attribute this uneasiness to a vague air of distraction in the class. If only he could put his finger on the trouble! The thought then occurred to him that there might be something wrong with himself. Finally it came to him — he was still cold. Perplexed, he turned and put his hand close to the stove. He touched it with his finger tips, gingerly at first, then laying his palm flat on the smooth top. It was stone cold! Amazed, he raised the lid and peered inside. Down at the bottom lay a grayish mass of crinkled, burned paper, over small pieces of kindling that still gleamed with dying sparks. On top of all this lay four or five large round objects blackened by the smoke. These had crushed out the fire.

Father Cugliero pushed his long arm into the stove to

pull up one of the objects — quickly drew it out again and blew vigorously on his fingers. He grabbed the poker and raked out one of them. It clattered noisily on the iron base in front of the stove. A stone! And the rest of the big gray-and-black objects that followed it — stones! The teacher glared at the class. They stared back at him in wide-eyed innocence.

"Who did this?" he asked quietly.

No one answered.

"Who did it?" he asked, this time in a roar.

Still no one answered, so he decided to go about his investigation more methodically.

"Who's responsible for the stove this week?"

"Savio!" everyone said.

"Savio?" cried the priest, hardly able to believe his ears. He shouted angrily, "Come up here, Savio!"

Dominic came up and stood before him.

"Who did this, Savio?"

No answer.

"Did you do it?"

Dominic refused to answer the priest's question and instead hung his head.

Father Cugliero's faith in human nature underwent a crisis. In that brief moment of silence, he recalled the wonderful impression he had received of Savio from what his friend, Father John, had said at the time of Dominic's First Communion. Why, Father John had built up the boy as a little saint! Perhaps he had been — then. He certainly must have changed since. Here he was, caught in a mean trick, and he did not even have the courage to own up to it. The little hypocrite!

"Savio," he said, slowly and deliberately, "I must confess that this is an unpleasant surprise for me, a very unpleasant surprise. I could hardly have believed it. If it had been anyone else I should have punished him severely. But it's the first time you have come before me. Kneel down there in the center of the class until I tell you to get up!"

Dominic went to the center of the room--and knelt down. He would continue to follow the classes in that position until recess. For the rest of the period the class was quieter than usual, even with the teacher present.

Before recess began, a group of boys approached the rostrum sheepishly and stood in front of Father Cugliero.

"Well?" he said, surprised to see a delegation.

One of the boys stepped forward. It was the one who had "fixed" the stove.

"Taintsaviosir!" he said hurriedly. His mouth was twitching.

"What did you say, boy?"

"He says: ' 'Tain't Savio, sir!' That's what he says, sir," ventured another boy.

"Please don't use that word ' 'Tain't' again. ' 'Tain't' is . . . Oh well! Now what is it that isn't Savio?"

"Savio didn't put the stones in the fire, sir."

"What? Savio didn't! Then who did?"

"Don't know, sir. Only Savio didn't, sir."

Father Cugliero glared at the faces staring at him over the desk. They didn't know who it was, but they knew it wasn't Savio. How very odd! He decided, nevertheless, not to press the point. Instead, he dismissed the boys and called Dominic up again.

"Savio, was it you who put the stones in the stove?"

Dominic again hung his head in silence.

But this time Father Cugliero insisted.

"Answer me, yes or no, Savio. Was it you?"

"No, sir."

"Then why on earth did you not say so at first? I'd soon have found the culprit and . . ."

"Well, sir, the one who did it was already on his last chance, and if you'd found it out, you'd have sent him home. It would only have been my first chance and I knew you'd let me off with something lighter. Besides," he added, lowering his eyes, "I thought of our Lord when *He* was unjustly accused. *He* didn't say a word either."

Father Cugliero was immensely relieved for a moment at the boy's explanation. Then he grew even more indignant than before, not at Dominic this time, but at the others who had allowed Dominic to suffer for the trick they had played on him.

"Do you know what I'll do?" he said, breathing rather heavily. "I'll get the name of everyone who had a hand in this business and I'll . . ."

"Father," interrupted Dominic, "do you think you could let them go — just this once?"

Dominic smiled and put all the appeal he could muster into his entreaty. He would have suffered more than the boys if they had been punished.

Father Cugliero looked at him for a moment, and then fought back the smile on his own face.

"Well," he answered as gruffly as he could, "since it's for you. Just this once. But you won't save them the next time."

CHAPTER 5

GARMENT FOR GOD

FATHER CUGLIERO never forgot the incident of the stove. It made him realize that there was something deep and strong in Dominic. One day, while he was thinking of the boy, by coincidence he received a letter telling him that Don Bosco would be coming to keep the Feast of the Rosary at his native village, Becchi, which was about a half-hour's walk from Moriondo.

Don Bosco's fame had spread all over Piedmont by this time. His earlier trials and setbacks were no longer remembered, and he was fast becoming an influential figure in the State as well as in the Church. Father Cugliero knew this. He also knew, however, that like everybody else, Don Bosco was extremely fond of his own native countryside, and was always interested in hearing about Becchi and its inhabitants. Father Cugliero read Don Bosco's letter and, impulsive as he was, at once decided to go to Turin, see Don Bosco, and talk to him about young Savio. Then, when Don Bosco came to

Becchi, he would send Dominic to meet him, and leave the rest to God.

One day in early October, therefore, Father Cugliero put on his round, broad-brimmed clerical hat, gathered up the tails of his cassock, and boarded the coach for Turin.

"You may have a number of excellent boys here as you say, Don Bosco, but I don't think you could possibly have any better than young Savio. Try him out and see if you don't find in him another St. Aloysius." This was the substance of a long tribute paid to Dominic by Father Cugliero upon his arrival in Turin.

Don Bosco could not help smiling at Father Cugliero's enthusiasm.

"All right, Father," said the saint. "I hope you're right. I'll be at Becchi for the Feast of the Rosary. Suppose you send him up to see me then?"

"I'll make sure he goes, Don Bosco."

On his return to Mondonio, the teacher sent for Dominic.

"Would you like to go to school in Turin, Dominic?"

"That would be wonderful, Father!"

"Well . . . you're going!"

"Gee, that's great! . . . But how about the money, Father?"

"Suppose we let Providence look after that?"

"Oh, then . . ."

Dominic remembered "the lots of money needed to be a priest" and a doubt remained in his mind. Shortly afterward he approached his teacher again and asked, "Are you sure, Father, that our Lord Himself is looking after the money part?"

"Get out of here, you doubting Thomas!" Father Cugliero roared.

The month of the Rosary was hardly started when word flashed around Mondonio: Don Bosco was at Becchi!

As soon as Dominic heard the news, he set off with his father early one Monday morning, October 2, 1854, for an interview. Like the rest of the people in the region, Dominic had heard the usual stories about the saint. He could see through you, he could tell you what you were thinking, he could work miracles . . . and yet, despite all the wonderful things that Dominic had heard, he felt perfectly at ease in Don Bosco's presence. Usually so reserved and almost reticent with strangers, Dominic dropped all his reserve and spoke as frankly to the saint as if they had been old friends.

"What's your name, son?"

"Dominic Savio, Father."

"Where from?"

"Moriondo, Father. Father Cugliero said he spoke to you about me."

"Yes, he did indeed. How are your studies?"

Dominic told him. What he said was borne out by his father, who added proudly that his son knew the Catechism by heart.

As was his constant habit, Don Bosco gradually brought the conversation around to the state of the other's soul. Their talk took on an air of cordial intimacy.

"We were soon in each other's confidence," wrote Don Bosco. "He in mine, and I in his."

Toward the end of the interview, Dominic wanted to settle things definitely.

"Do you mean to let me come to the Oratory?" he asked the priest.

"Yes," Don Bosco smiled. "You see, I think I see in you a lot of good material."

"What do you think it's good for, Father?"

"To make a beautiful garment for our Lord."

"So I'm going to be the cloth . . . you the tailor?"

"Precisely. Only . . ."

"Only what?"

"Well, to tell the truth, Dominic, you don't seem to be any too strong."

"Oh, don't mind that, Don Bosco! God will give me enough for the future."

"And when you finish your studies, what would you like to be?"

"A priest. If God gives me strength enough, Father, I should like to be a priest."

"Fine. Fine!" exclaimed Don Bosco. "Now, Dominic, I want to see how much that head of yours will hold."

He picked up a little volume of his own *Catholic Readings.*

"Take this book and learn this page by heart. Tomorrow when you have it down pat, come and see me again. Meanwhile you can take some fresh air and let your father and myself discuss the ways and means of sending you to the Oratory."

The priest turned to Dominic's father. "Now, Mr. Savio . . ."

Details concerning Dominic's departure were discussed

and about eight minutes later they were finished. Dominic reappeared in the doorway.

"Excuse me, Father, but if you want to hear that lesson now . . ."

"Mind you, Dominic," warned Don Bosco, "I meant you to learn it by heart!"

"I know, Father, and still I'm ready."

"So soon? Very well. Let's hear it."

"When a man considers the value of his soul . . ." Dominic sailed through the lesson with one or two stops for breath. He followed up a brilliant performance with explanations of what he had memorized.

"Bravo!" exclaimed Don Bosco in genuine surprise. "Bravo, indeed!"

All three were smiling.

Don Bosco looked at Dominic for a moment. His piercing blue eyes searched the boy's face.

"Dominic," he said at last, "since you anticipated the lesson, I'll anticipate my answer. From this very moment, I count you as one of Don Bosco's boys. You must start praying from now on that you and I may do God's holy will in your regard."

Dominic took the priest's large leathery hand in his own small white ones and kissed it warmly. Don Bosco blessed both him and his father and the two set out again along the road to Moriondo.

This meeting, incidentally, took place at the humble Bosco home in Becchi. Afterward Don Bosco used to point out to his friends exactly where he and Dominic stood while they had talked together. After that first meeting he wrote this impression of the boy: "A cheerful youngster with a smiling face . . . I recognized in him a soul made wholly according to the spirit of God, and I was not a little astonished to see the marvels that grace had already wrought in one so young."

CHAPTER 6

BIG CITY

It was the morning of October 29, 1854, and Dominic, after serving Father Cugliero's Mass for the last time, said good-by. Arriving home, he found that a strange quiet had descended on the house.

"Somebody dead?" he asked, in an attempt to dispel the gloom.

"Eat plenty, son," said his father, "you have a long day ahead."

Dominic's mother did not speak.

"Dominic, mommy and daddy were crying because you're going away," Raimonda said.

After that Dominic did not dare speak. He began to eat the substantial meal his mother had prepared for him, new bread, grapes and pears, three thick slices of salami. But his mouth was dry and he had to gulp down each morsel half-chewed. At last he gave up trying.

"I have no appetite," he said. "Maybe it's too early."

Final preparations were hurried so they would not miss

the coach to Turin. At last his luggage was ready: a wooden case containing all his extra clothing and the few gifts that some friends had brought him when they heard he was going to Don Bosco's Oratory. There was a new pair of breeches, two pairs of heavy, striped woolen stockings, and a sturdy pair of boots. The second piece of luggage was a bundle containing a warm blanket and odd articles of clothing wrapped up in sackcloth and sewed together with twine.

The sad good-bys were said. Dominic's father took up the box, Dominic placed the bundle under his arm, and they both set out for the road where the coach would pass. On board the coach, it was only after Charles Savio had awkwardly but gently dried his son's eyes several times with his large red handkerchief that Dominic sat up. After a deep, shaking sigh or two of the kind that people give when they have wept for a long time, he began to take notice of his whereabouts.

The vehicle they rode in was a two-horse carriage called a "speed-car." When the old folks saw these "speed-cars" rushing along the country roads at 20 miles an hour, they wondered if almighty God had ever intended man to travel at such speed! There were no railroads as yet in Italy except the one that ran southward from Turin to Genoa. The Turin-Chieri line that Dominic would have taken was not inaugurated until 1874, twenty years later. The "speed-car" carried Dominic through Chieri, where Don Bosco had studied for the priesthood, climbed over Pino Hill, crossed the river Po, and entered Turin from the east.

On the way to Turin, Charles Savio drew his son's

attention from his sad thoughts by pointing out to him the fields of corn, maize, and grass; the scattered poplars, willows, mulberry bushes for silkworm feed; above all the rows and rows of vines that stood like walls, and could hide a man as he walked between them. Hamlets, villages, towns were all around, some in the shelter of a valley, others on the side of a hill or even on top of one — an ancient precaution against attack — but protected from the rough winds by thick circles of acacia trees.

As the carriage rolled into Turin, the sights of the city streets held Dominic's attention until the driver *whoad* his horses to a halt at Castle Place.

The city of Turin, at the time when Dominic saw it, was not a quiet city. In fact, it was a city in an uproar.

Italy, up to now, had been just a number of states into which it had been broken up when the Roman Empire fell. These states were so independent they even went to war against each other. Powerful outsiders — Spain, France, and Austria, for example — then stepped in and marched up and down the country so often, as if they owned the place, that the Italians at last decided it was time to do something about it. They planned to rise together, form one solid nation, and chase out the invader. Sometimes, because of the danger, they could not work out in the open. Then they formed secret societies and worked under cover. These societies had names like the *Mafia, Carbonari,* and the *Camorra.*

The little kingdom of Piedmont in the north of Italy was the rallying point of the movement for independence. Turin was the capital of Piedmont, and it naturally became the center of the revolution. When Dominic arrived it was filled with soldiers, revolutionaries, statesmen, and politicians.

Dominic was thrilled as he walked beside his father along the broad, airy streets of Turin.

What added to the thrill was the sight of the soldiers walking the streets singly, in groups, or marching behind a military band in columns on the roadway. There were so many of them in Turin during those days they seemed to double the city's usual population of 160,000. To be exact, though, no more than 15,000 men under General Alfonso La Marmora were billeted in the city.

Fascinated by the sight of the shining leather belt, the cordon and tassels, and the gallant waving plume of a passing soldier, Dominic stopped and stared. The soldier stopped, too, and smiled.

"Olà, sonny!" he called out to Dominic. "Want to become a soldier."

"No, sir," Dominic replied, smiling back at him. "I want to become a saint."

Had Dominic possessed a sixth sense, he would have felt, as he neared the Oratory of Don Bosco, that he was walking on ground where a great many saints had already walked before him. Saints were now walking the same streets even in his own time! In spite of the toil and trouble that was then fermenting in the royal city, Turin in that period gave to the world an astonishing number of saints: St. John Bosco, St. Joseph Cafasso, St. Joseph Cottolengo, St. Mary Mazzarello, St. Dominic Savio, Venerable Don Rua . . .

As it happened, he was not even aware that when he passed the Carignano and the Madama buildings, the Parliament in the former and the Senate in the latter were busily rewriting the history of his country.

He kept walking beside his father until he came to a suburb of Turin called *Valdocco,* or "the valley of the slain saints." He saw the low, tiled wall that encircled a long, renovated old house. This was the "Oratory" where Don Bosco was doing so much for the poor children of Turin. In the beginning, it had been a source of astonishment and even scandal. Now it was attracting the favorable attention of northern Italy.

CHAPTER 7

SECRET ORDERS

WHO was Don Bosco?

What was the Oratory?

Since Don Bosco and the Oratory played the most important part in Dominic's life, it might be well to say a word about them at this point.

Don Bosco was Father John Bosco, the best friend the boys of Turin ever had. He was so fond of them he started looking around for a chance to do something big for them.

On the Feast of the Immaculate Conception, 1841, he was vesting for Mass. He heard a commotion at the door of the sacristy. Joe Camotti, the sacristan, was using strong-arm methods to put a boy out of the sacristy. Don Bosco did not like it.

He called out to the sacristan, "Joe! Joe!"

Joe came back, breathing heavily.

"What do you mean, Joe, by treating one of my friends like that?"

"One of your friends?" Joe was amazed. "Mean to tell me, Father, that that kid, dirty and cheeky, and lounging about my sacristy though he can't serve Mass, is one of your friends?"

"That's what I said, Joe. Call him back."

The boy came back, a little scared, and stood in front of Don Bosco, twisting an old cap in his hands.

"What's your name, son?"

"Bart Garelli."

In answer to Don Bosco's questions Bart said he had no home, no father nor mother, no job, no education.

"Can you sing, Bart?" said Don Bosco, fishing around for a contact.

"You kiddin', Father?"

"Whistle?"

Bart grinned sheepishly. He laughed openly when he saw Don Bosco laughing.

"Like to come up to our club?" Don Bosco asked.

"Sure would, Father." Bart was now completely at his ease.

"How about next Sunday?"

"Suits me."

Bart came next Sunday and brought some friends with him. The number of boys grew and grew and Don Bosco had to find new quarters for them. Up to now the club had moved from place to place. The quarters would have to be permanent this time. Don Bosco tried and tried and finally gave up.

He sat down one day in a field surrounded by the boys. Everybody was very sad. Don Bosco told them that if God wanted the work to go on, He Himself would have to do something to keep it going, for Don Bosco had done all that lay in his power.

A man walked up and said that he had a place for sale. It was in a tough part of town. Don Bosco didn't mind. People were never tough with him. Don Bosco asked friends for the money, bought the place, and called it the "Oratory." Boys at the Oratory were to have a chance to live good, clean lives. They were to have a chance even to become saints. Don Bosco always believed that boys would want to become nothing less than saints, if only things were explained to them in the right way.

He decided that now was the time to start a hostel where his boys could sleep instead of sleeping in the streets. The first boys he took in ran away with the blankets and the bed sheets. He tried again. This time the idea caught on and the number of his boys grew.

Don Bosco taught the boys to read and write and taught them trades. He went out and found jobs for them. He found places for them at good schools free of charge. He brought his own mother down from the country to look after them.

He gave up so much for his boys people began to think he was crazy. They said he ought to be locked up for his own good, and one day they sent two persons down to take him away in a carriage. Don Bosco smiled at the maneuvers. He insisted politely that the two envoys get into the carriage before him. When they were inside, he stepped back and slammed the carriage door.

"To the asylum!" he cried to the poor, confused driver. "And for heaven's sake, don't stop along the way! You have two dangerous characters on board!"

The local police got after him. No sane man, they

said, would mix up with a bunch of hoodlums, as they
called Don Bosco's boys. Not unless there was something
afoot. One policeman thought he had found the answer:
Don Bosco was starting up another secret society! This
police officer gave Don Bosco a lot of trouble. Then one
day he thought he had discovered Don Bosco's secret
orders from the Vatican. There was a great to-do until
Don Bosco showed the "secret orders" to the searchers.
They were food bills for the Oratory.

At the Oratory, Don Bosco kept things as simple as
possible. There was a minimum of discipline. For instance, the boys were supposed to come to Mass in the
morning, but no one was there to see whether they came.
To check their attendance, each one inserted a little
wooden peg opposite his name. A few of the bigger boys
helped run the Oratory.

At mealtimes they took their portions — usually bread
and a substantial soup or stew — and sat down wherever
they liked to eat it. The meal over, they washed their
own utensils and gathered around Don Bosco's chair
and talked to him. Don Bosco won their confidence, and
they accepted everything he said as coming from one
who had their happiness at heart.

Dominic arrived when there were about 80 to 100 boys
at the Oratory, all apprentices or students. Both groups
had to leave each morning to go to school or to work,
since Don Bosco was too poor to provide classrooms or
workshops for them. Dominic entered into this atmosphere of poverty and simplicity on October 10, 1854, and
found himself immediately at home.

CHAPTER 8

IN THE SERVICE OF THE QUEEN

DON BOSCO's quarters, to which Dominic and his father were conducted, were a barely furnished room in a poor-looking house. There was a well-worn writing desk, a bookcase, a kneeler, and an extra chair for visitors. The furniture covers were shabby and the wood was chipped around the edges; the stole hanging over the kneeler was a faded purple on one side, and a dingy white on the other. Since there was only one extra chair in the room, Dominic had to stand.

Don Bosco recognized them immediately. After a few inquiries about affairs at Becchi and Mondonio, he spoke to Dominic. Dominic kept looking at the wall behind the desk.

"What's attracting your attention, Dominic?" Don Bosco asked.

"That sign, Father."

"Oh, that!" exclaimed Don Bosco. "Don't tell me you know some Latin already!"

"Yes, Father, a little. Since I want to be a priest, I asked Father Cugliero to teach me."

"Go ahead. Try your hand at that."

"Well, *da* means *give*. That's easy. *Mihi* means *to me*, and *animas* means er . . . ah . . ."

"Sooo . . ." prompted Don Bosco, smiling.

"Oh, yes, *souls! Da mihi animas:* Give me souls."

"What about the next?" asked Don Bosco.

"*Caetera tolle* . . . Boy! That's something! *Caetera tolle* . . . Guess I can't make it, Father." Dominic blushed when he said this.

"Well, I suppose it is hard. I'll help you. *Caetera* means *the rest. Tolle* means *take away*. So the whole thing says: Give me souls; take away the rest!"

"What a beautiful motto!"

"It's a kind of contract, Dominic. I give everything to God and He, in return, gives me souls. I took it from a saint I'm fond of, St. Francis of Sales."

As soon as Dominic settled down to his new life, Don Bosco decided that, like the other students, he should go outside to continue his studies. Since there was no provision yet for the boys to study at the Oratory, Don Bosco had searched Turin until he found some teachers willing to take his boys free of charge. He did the same for the apprentices and always made sure that they were placed in safe hands. He visited the boys regularly at study or work and checked up on their conduct and progress.

Professor Bonzanino conducted classes in the lower grades for the children of the wealthy families in the city. So convinced was he of the importance of Don Bosco's work, he willingly accepted, without fee, a number of the more promising boys from the Oratory. Dominic was chosen to attend the Professor's school.

Dominic made an excellent impression at this school. By nature he was polite, and as neat in dress as his circumstances would allow. This he had learned at home, for the Savios were noted for their sense of decency. Dominic never showed signs of being embarrassed by his poverty in such elegant surroundings, nor was he ever ashamed to introduce his poorly dressed father to the rest of the boys — not the usual thing at his age. Neither his poverty nor the position of authority he later enjoyed prevented him and the others from becoming friends.

Professor Bonzanino soon learned to place the more troublesome boys of the class near Dominic. He became convinced, after trial, that this was sufficient to induce a notable change in any wayward boy. Finally, Dominic became his assistant, and whenever the Professor had to absent himself from class, he left it understood that Dominic was in charge.

Some amusing stories are told of Dominic and the poor Oratory boys among their wealthier school companions. At the Oratory, for instance, each boy had his own knife, fork, and spoon, for which he was responsible. One day, during class, a fork fell out of one boy's pocket. The others were amused at this and asked him if he always carried hardware in his pocket.

"Think I'd have it long if I left it at home?" the boy replied. He was as amazed at their suggestion as they were at his answer.

When winter came, Don Bosco distributed a number of military capes he had been given by the Army for his boys. The capes were wonderfully warm but not very stylish. When the Oratory boys appeared at school in them, Professor Bonzanino, with kindly understanding, gave them a separate room where they could hang the soldiers' capes away from the elegant overcoats of the others. It was bad enough with their wooden clogs that clattered through the classrooms.

When asked what impression he had formed of Dominic during the boy's stay with him, the Professor wrote this neat little description of his pupil: "In the care of his hair and dress, Savio was not at all affected, but in his humble condition, he appeared to be clean, well mannered, and courteous. So much so, that his companions, even those of noble birth, were delighted to be with him, not only because of his knowledge and piety, but also for his pleasant ways and general ability."

It was not long before someone in the Oratory began to notice that Dominic, though like the rest of the better boys in many ways, was still different from them in many others. This was Don Bosco's mother. Mama Margaret had been as much responsible for the sanctity of her son as her son was to be for the sanctity of Dominic.

"Believe me, John," she said, "you have many good boys at the Oratory, but Dominic, I'm convinced, is going to top them all."

Don Bosco pretended to be surprised.

"Yes indeed, John," she insisted. "It's written on almost everything he does. Inside the church he's like an angel, and outside he seems always to be in the presence of God."

Dominic was, in time, promoted to the higher classes of Professor Father Pico, another admirer of Don Bosco's work. He conducted a school much like Professor Bonzanino's, but for more advanced students. This new professor later said of Dominic: "I think I see him now as he used to come into my class, with that modest bearing so characteristic of him. . . . Even to see Dominic made people stop and wish to speak to him." To Professor Pico, Dominic was always "the little saint."

These estimates of Dominic's character were not made fifty years after his death, when no one then alive could call them into question. Three days after Dominic's death, Father Pico invited his boys to disprove the claims he had made of the sanctity of Savio. No one accepted the invitation. The things that Don Bosco wrote about Dominic were also written immediately after the young saint's death. They could easily have been verified by those who knew Dominic intimately.

Soon after the boy's death, Don Bosco issued a general invitation for anyone to come forward who had noticed anything unbecoming in Dominic's conduct. No one did so. He closed the inquiry by declaring: "All those who knew him were unanimous in saying that they could find nothing in him to merit correction. They could not even suggest what might have been added to the sum of his good qualities."

He concluded with a remark that is an important indication of the type of boy Dominic was: "His cheerful character and lively disposition made him extremely popular, even among those boys who were no great lovers of their Faith."

It does seem strange that long before Dominic's death, the saint should have set himself the task of preparing material for the boy's biography. But according to Pope Pius XI, with Don Bosco "the miraculous had become almost the ordinary." He, therefore, probably foresaw the future glory of his pupil and intended to leave the evidence needed for his Cause of Canonization.

He also saw in Dominic his own idea of what he thought a Catholic boy should be. Whatever he urged his boys to do, he saw that Dominic was trying to do it no matter how much trouble or pain it caused him. For instance, Don Bosco insisted that a Catholic boy should always have a clean mind and live a clean life. And nobody at the Oratory had a cleaner mind or lived a cleaner life than Dominic. Perhaps Don Bosco even dreamed of making Dominic the ideal of every Catholic classroom round the world.

Since Don Bosco was a great friend of boys, he was continually on the lookout for ways to help them. Perhaps that is why he sat down to write the life of Dominic even before the other died. And every time he had to look over a fresh edition of his best seller, *The Life of Dominic Savio*, the boys of the Oratory always found him openly and unashamedly in tears.

That year, 1854, Dominic made the novena to the Immaculate Conception with special fervor. Each day of the novena his love for the Mother of God increased until finally he could no longer hold himself in. He felt he had to speak to somebody about what was on his mind, and with Dominic that somebody always meant Don

Bosco. In the evening, therefore, when Don Bosco was accustomed to receive his boys, he knocked at the saint's door.

"Father," he said, "I should like to do something very special for our Lady during this Novena."

"An excellent idea, Dominic," said Don Bosco.

"Yes," replied Dominic. "But what do you think I ought to do?"

"Nothing but your duty," said Don Bosco. "Although you might pay particular attention to your prayers."

"I'd like to do something more than that."

"Then go often to Holy Communion."

"I'm doing that already, Don Bosco," said Dominic. "Soon I hope to be able to go every day. But I'd still like to do something more."

"What then?"

"I'd first like to make a general confession, then offer myself completely to our Lady and ask her to keep me from sin. You see, I want the grace to be allowed to die before I ever commit a mortal sin."

December 8, 1854, was a day of great public rejoicing for Catholics around the world, for the Holy Father, Pope Pius IX, proclaimed the dogma of the Immaculate Conception.

That evening, in a quiet corner of the Oratory church, Dominic knelt at the altar of the Mother of God and consecrated himself completely to her service for the rest of his life. He repeated to her his heroic motto: Death before sin!

"From this moment," wrote Don Bosco, "began that

exemplary kind of life, that exactness in the performance of his duty, beyond which it is difficult to go."

He was only twelve and a half years old, and this was his second important step along the road to sanctity.

CHAPTER 9

HUNTER OF SOULS

"THE first thing to remember in saving one's own soul is to look to the souls of others."

This was one of the earliest lessons Dominic learned from Don Bosco. It had been the basis of the saint's whole system of life, and had earned for him the title of "hunter of souls." Dominic, in his turn, made it the mainspring of his activity. He tried to imitate Don Bosco even in the means he used to approach the souls of others.

Dominic was always good-natured and helpful. The smile rarely left his determined little mouth. When a long-laid siege to bring some wanderer back to the fold brought nothing more than insulting words and blows, the smile persisted and left the way open for another attempt.

The two great pillars on which Dominic founded his one-man Catholic Action program were Confession and Communion. These also gave him a neat formula for a happy life. "What more can I want to make me happy?" he used to say. "If I have something that troubles me,

Sanctuary of Church of St. Francis de Sales, Turin, where Dominic consecrated his life to our Lady.

Shed, converted by Don Bosco for his Oratory.
From a painting of the Pinardi.

Old communal school at Castelnuovo.

I go to Confession and — pouf! — it's gone! If I need a special favor, I simply go to Holy Communion and — paff! — I get it!"

Following the example set by his master, who sought souls wherever they were to be found, in season and out of season, Dominic also went after souls in the highways and byways of his own little world.

The most important field of Dominic's operations, the Oratory, was, we have seen, somewhat more complex than a mere boarding school. In 1856–1857, there were about 170 boarders there and they formed an oddly mixed group. First, there were the students, a more or less quiet group of boys who followed a regular course of study; then there were the apprentices — less manageable, and wise to many of the world's ways; later there were the day-boys who came to classes at the Oratory as soon as they were opened. Besides these, there were boys of all ages and conditions — six or seven hundred at that time — who came in from the neighboring streets on Sundays and feast days for the fun and games they enjoyed after Catechism.

Among these boys Dominic found plenty of scope for his Catholic Action. Of course, like the others, he enjoyed being at the Oratory on Sundays and holidays because the general atmosphere, with its noise and bustle, was that of a fair day. But he always kept an eye out for business — his Father's business.

His most profitable moments were during the games. It was one of Dominic's favorite tricks to pick out a boy who was "not a saint," and shift the positions on the teams so that he got near the boy either as a partner or as an opponent. He would use every trick he knew to turn the conversation around to the soul or to confession. Then, preferably during a break in the game, he would shoot his arrow.

"Say, now that we're on the subject — how about going to Confession together? Would Saturday suit you?"

Sometimes the other would agree offhandedly, just to free himself from Dominic's insistence.

"O.K.! O.K.! Whatever you say. Next Saturday. All right. Now let's get on with the game."

On that slender thread of a halfhearted promise Dominic would hold him. By Saturday, of course, the boy would have forgotten all about it. Suddenly Dominic would appear to remind him of his promise and lead him off, protesting, to Confession.

Occasionally it did not quite work out that way. Perhaps the boy would remember his promise in time to clear out of Dominic's sight. After a long and fruitless search, Dominic would give up trying to find his friend, at least for that day. But if Dominic found him later, when the boy thought that Dominic had forgotten about the promise, the conversation usually ran something like this.

"Ah! So there you are, my friend!"

"Oh! Hi, Dom! You know, I was . . . ah . . . sick that time I was to come up to see you."

"Poor kid! Maybe you were sick because you had something on your mind. Why not go to Confession and get rid of it? How about Saturday?"

After this double dose, the boy would usually give up.

"Do you want many graces?" Dominic would ask the

other boys. "Go and visit the Blessed Sacrament often. Do you want few graces? Visit the Blessed Sacrament rarely. Do you want none at all? Then never pay a visit to the Blessed Sacrament."

Dominic believed this wholeheartedly. He wanted his companions to make a habit of paying frequent visits to the Blessed Sacrament, and whenever he himself went in, he always tried to get someone to go with him. To make it easier for the boys to pay these short visits, Don Bosco had built the chapel near the playground. They could pop in and out whenever they felt like it.

Even on vacation, Dominic carried the spirit of the apostle with him. He found it easy to do so at home because of his prestige. Anyone who studied in the big city of Turin enjoyed a certain reputation. The neighbors knew him as the boy who never cared to play or talk in choir, but preferred to pray at our Lady's altar. Had it been anyone else his companions might have made him suffer for it, but Dominic — well, they liked Dominic and expected him to act as he did.

There was nothing spectacular about Dominic's work at home. Counting the baby boy who died before Dominic was born, and the sister who was born after Dominic's death, there were in all eleven children in the family. Dominic would tell his younger brothers and sisters some of the stories he had heard at the Oratory, and describe the wonderful things he had seen in Turin — throwing in a moral the way Don Bosco had told him.

He always came home well supplied with religious medals and holy pictures. These he gave out as prizes to the smaller boys and girls who could make the Sign of the Cross, answer questions from the Catechism, or recite the prayers.

"Hi, Bruno!" he said to one little boy with big brown eyes. "Want a medal?"

"Sure, I wanna medal, Dominic. Gimme it."

Bruno waited for the handout.

"You can have the medal, Bruno, if you can tell me why God made you."

"Sure I can tell you why God made me. God made me . . . God made me to love Him and . . . and . . ."

A shadow of anxiety crept into Bruno's eyes, and tears threatened.

Dominic came to the rescue before the tears could flow.

"Well, Bruno, if you can tell me that God made you to love, honor, and serve Him in this life, and be happy with Him in the next — I guess you'll earn the medal just the same."

After this refresher course, the child got the medal and probably never again forgot why God made little Bruno.

Dominic was a good storyteller, too, and on Sunday afternoons he would gather the children of the village around him. They would sit under a tree in the fields if it was warm, or in the barn if it was cold, and listen, as children of all ages love to listen, to a good story.

One of the most touching incidents in the whole of Dominic's career — "career" is the only word to describe his attitude toward sainthood — is the one that concerns a boy he met who refused to go to church.

Dominic was on his way to Mass at the time. The bitter wind sliced at his ankles and in through the opening of his overcoat. He snuggled his chin deeper into the folds of his muffler.

He had already passed through the church doorway when he stopped. His mind began to work in reverse. Someone was back there, stalling, and it was time for Mass. He turned and walked back.

"Hello!" he said.

"Hello!" said the boy. He was poorly dressed and stood against the wall. He held his elbows close to his sides with the cold.

"Going to Mass?"

"No."

"Er . . . don't you . . . Why won't you go? Are you sick?"

"No."

"Are you cold?"

"You said it, brother! Freezin'! Bin cold all day."

"You'd be warmer in church."

"Maybe."

"Then why don't you go in?"

"Just don't feel like it."

"But why? Can't you tell me?"

"Guess so. I'm . . . you see . . . I'm ashamed to go in these clothes. My coat's torn and my pants is torn, too. If I turned around you could see 'em."

"Oh, I'm sorry! . . . Tell you what. If you wear this big coat of mine nobody will see your coat and it's long enough to hide your pants — that is, if you don't pull it up and you don't bend down. Try it on, just to see. There! What did I tell you!"

"Boy! Looks swell, don't it?"

"Sure does. Let's go in."

"Say! What about you? Your coat . . ."

"Come on! Let's go! We're late as it is."

This time a warm coat, another time a pair of gloves, a third time a share of his food . . . these things mattered very little to Dominic. What mattered much more was to be able to help others.

For all his zeal, Dominic seems to have been blessed with more than a grain of common sense. This told him whether or not his interference would do any good.

One afternoon while coming from school with a friend, Dominic was passing a teamster driving a wagon. Just at that moment the horse began to balk. The teamster tried everything he knew to make the horse move, including a blistering stream of profanity. Dominic blushed, raised his hat, and murmured something to himself.

"What are you doing, Dominic?" his companion asked. "And what did you say to yourself?"

"Didn't you hear that man?" said Dominic. "He took our Lord's name in vain! If it would have been of any use I'd have gone up and spoken to him. But that might only have made it worse, so I raised my cap and said: Praised be Jesus Christ!"

Under the circumstances, faced with a rough teamster who was angry and on his way home from a hard day's work, there was not much else that Dominic, with prudence, could do.

He never hesitated, however, when he felt that he could do some good. On another occasion, for example, he was passing an elderly, well-dressed man who happened to drop a package in the gutter. The old gentleman was annoyed and began to use some very ungentlemanly language. Dominic was more horrified this time than he was with the poor working man. Here was one who, to all appearances, should have known better.

Dominic approached him with his usual smile.

"Excuse me, sir, I wonder if you could please do me a favor?"

"Of course, my little man! What is it?"

"Could you direct me to the Oratory of Don Bosco?"

"Why surely! Now listen carefully: You go straight ahead until you reach Queen Margaret Boulevard. Then . . ." The man gave him clear and precise instructions on how to reach the Oratory.

When he had finished, Dominic asked again, "Do you think you could do me another favor, sir?"

"If I have done you one favor so easily, I suppose I can do you another. What is it?"

"Do you think you could stop swearing?"

"What? Stop swearing? Well, upon my soul! To think that! — " the man spluttered.

He looked down at Dominic, knowing that by right he should feel offended. If any other young upstart had dared to say such a thing, he'd have known how to deal with him. He could not, however, become angry with this slip of a boy before him. He stared for a moment in amazement at Dominic, and then the lines about his eyes slowly fanned out into a smile.

"Well! Well! Well!" he said, this time in amusement. "You are perfectly right, my son. I really must stop this terrible habit I have of using bad language, and by . . . and I might as well begin right now!"

CHAPTER 10

IN THE LINE OF FIRE

WHEN Dominic had been at the Oratory long enough to become definitely established as an apostle, he made it his duty to look for boys that he thought he could help in one way or another. With this in mind, he once made friends with John Roda. Roda was an apprentice bricklayer who lived at the Oratory, and went out each day to work. He was not, as he himself confessed, "another St. Aloysius." For this reason, Don Bosco quietly handed him over to Dominic, hoping in this way to bring about a much-needed change. Roda himself tells what happened:

"When I first came to the Oratory, Don Bosco handed me over to the care of Dominic Savio. He was to show me around, said Don Bosco, and get me lined up with the routine of the place. During one of the very first days, I was playing bowls with him. I missed an easy shot and I was so darned mad I let fly a string of oaths. I picked up the habit knocking around the streets. You see, I never had any training or education. I no sooner opened my mouth than Dominic shouted in surprise. He came up and talked to me in an honest-to-goodness way. I was convinced I had to do something about it. So I hunted up Don Bosco and made a good Confession. I did exactly what Savio said and from that day to this, I have never fallen into the habit again. It's also to Savio I owe the fact that I went to the Sacraments. When I first came to the Oratory I didn't know a prayer, and I hadn't even once been to the Sacraments."

Another boy with the habit of swearing, who fell under the spell of Dominic, was a little fellow of nine years, called Thomas. Dominic overheard him swearing in a game with some companions.

"Tom," he called out to the youngster.

"Hello, Dom. Want me?"

"Yes, Tom." Dominic had an impulse to make Tom's ears as hot as his tongue. "I've found something you really ought to see. Follow me."

Filled with curiosity, Tom followed Dominic along corridors and up and down stairs. All the time Dominic kept making various signs to indicate some great secret. Finally, they turned into the Oratory church.

"There you are, Tom!"

Tom stared.

"Church?" he asked, without enthusiasm.

"Sure. You've got to tell the priest that you were swearing."

Realizing he had been tricked, Tom tried to find a loophole.

"But . . . but . . . I forget the Act of Contrition!"

"You forget the Act of Contrition!" Dominic seemed amazed. "Never mind. I'll help you out. Let's go through it together. 'Oh, my God, I am sorry . . .'"

"Oh, my God, I am sorry . . ."

Don Bosco declared in writing: "The thing that horrified Dominic and that caused not a little damage to his health, was to hear others swearing or taking the name of God in vain." If it hurt him so much, reasoned Dominic, it must hurt God a lot more. Therefore it was up to him to do his best to stop it.

Another time, Dominic was returning from school when he noticed the straight, well-built figure of a soldier ahead of him. The soldier was standing, evidently waiting for someone. As Dominic came up to the soldier, a little bell tinkled and out of a side street a priest approached, returning from a sick call. According to the custom of the time, since the priest carried the Blessed Sacrament in public, he was wearing a surplice and a humeral veil. Two altar boys escorted him with lighted candles.

When the Blessed Sacrament came near, Dominic knelt down on the wet pavement. The soldier, however, remained on his feet and pretended not to see the boy.

"Won't you kneel down, sir?" asked Dominic. "It's the Blessed Sacrament, you know."

"No," said the soldier shortly. "How can I kneel in these?" As if to excuse himself, he pointed to his well-pressed trousers.

Dominic said nothing, but took out his handkerchief and spread it on the ground. Then he looked up at the soldier again and smiled. "Won't you kneel down now?"

The soldier blushed, but in the end knelt down at

Dominic's side until the Blessed Sacrament had passed.

One of the most dramatic events in Dominic's career of Catholic Action must certainly have been that of the stone duel.

Two of the Oratory boys attending the outside classes of Professor Bonzanino one day had a quarrel. One of them insulted the family of the other. Ordinarily, among boys who had been taken off the streets by Don Bosco, this would have caused no trouble. Perhaps, however, they had seen how the boys of rich families reacted to such offenses and they, too, decided that the insult offered to their family honor would have to be wiped out with blood. They challenged each other to the only kind of duel with which they were familiar — a duel with stones. This duel with stones was no light matter. It was an ugly business in which serious hurts could be inflicted.

When Dominic heard of their plan, he first wrote letters to them and tried in every way he could to make them change their minds. It was no use telling Don Bosco, for the boys could easily pick the time and place to please themselves and no one would ever know.

"Tell you what," suggested Dominic finally. "Let me know where you're going to fight so I can come and see it."

"Sure, sure!" said one of the boys. "Wouldn't that be just dandy! We tell you, you tell Don Bosco, and then you both come along and break it up!"

"No; I don't mean it that way. I promise not to tell anyone else, and you know I always keep a promise."

Dominic, by the way, never broke that promise, even after the event. What happened was told to Don Bosco

later by one of the duelists himself. This boy also spoke
of the terrible feeling that came over him on witnessing
Dominic's action on the morning of the duel.

While waiting for the duel, Dominic felt very much
upset. Apparently he was disturbed, not only by the
thought of the harm that might come to one or the other,
but also by the thought that both of them were now living
in hatred of each other, and were, therefore, in a state
of mortal sin.

The day of the duel came and Dominic saw the two
boys heading for the appointed meeting place. He followed them and tried one last time to get them to make
up. He was told to save his breath.

"If you won't give up the duel," he insisted, "then at
least accept a condition."

"What condition?"

"I'll tell you when we get there," Dominic said.

The others shrugged their shoulders. They were not
interested.

The two boys left for the spot they had selected. Dominic watched as each one took a dozen stones and placed
them in a pile at his feet. The duelists stood about twenty
paces apart, peeled off their jackets, and faced each other.
One look at those angry faces and Dominic knew that the
stones thrown at the short distance of twenty yards could
be murderous. Both chose a stone for the opening throw.
Then they turned to Dominic, the only other one present,
to give the signal. Dominic, aware that they were waiting
for him, was fumbling in his pockets.

"Don't forget," he called out meanwhile. "I have a
condition to lay down."

His hand came out of his pocket holding a metal object. He stepped directly into the line of fire and held up a crucifix.

"Start throwing!" he shouted.

"Get out of there, Dominic!" cried one boy. "You'll get killed!"

Dominic's eyes grew bright and he seemed to brace himself. Then he rushed over to the bigger boy.

"Here's the condition," he said. "You've got to throw the first stone at me and say: Christ died innocent and pardoned His enemies, but I want my revenge."

This knocked the boy off his balance.

"But . . . but I don't have anything against you, Dominic. Why I'd sock the guy that'd hurt you!"

Dominic went up to the other boy.

"All right then, you go first."

"Aw, gosh, Dominic!" said the second boy. "I can't throw at you! You don't come into this! . . ."

Dominic then spoke warmly to both of them and showed them how foolish they were to act this way. In the end, he forced the boys to make up and shake hands and walked away from the field with a duelist on each arm.

Sculptors and painters have preserved the memory of Dominic standing in this position and holding up a crucifix. It reminds you of the splendid figure of the great apostle, Francis Xavier, whom Dominic sought in his own little way to imitate.

More than once Dominic took deliberate risks in order to keep others away from an occasion of sin. Often these attempts, either because of bad timing on the part of Dominic, or because of bad temper on the part of the person concerned, would result in insults to him or even downright injury. When that happened, Dominic's only reaction was to keep perfect silence.

One winter day, when some of the boys were warming themselves around the only stove in the Oratory, the door opened softly.

Shuck! An outsize snowball missed its intended victim and flattened against the opposite wall.

"Hey!" someone inside shouted. "Don Bosco says you can't throw snowballs inside the rooms!"

Shuck! Shuck!

The boy outside was evidently not impressed by any ruling of Don Bosco, and kept up his snowballing. Dominic never let the rules be broken when he could do anything to prevent it, and he protested mildly to the offender.

"Don't do that," he said. "You know Don Bosco wouldn't like it."

At this the other entered the room and strode over to Dominic. He brought his open hand down twice. Two large red spots appeared on Dominic's face. The slaps were followed by a kick.

"Shut up, will you?" the boy shouted at Dominic. "And now run off and tell Don Bosco."

This was the second time that the same boy had attacked Dominic. The first time, Dominic had retaliated and the boys had stopped the fight. Now they waited to see what would happen. Dominic did not retaliate but simply turned back to the stove. The other boy, with an expression of contempt, wheeled around and walked with a swagger out of the room.

The name of the boy who had attacked Dominic was Ratazzi. He was a problem child and the nephew of a famous Government Minister. The Minister had asked Don Bosco to help the boy.

Young Ratazzi gave a lot of trouble at first, but the persistent kindly ways of Don Bosco and the example of Dominic and the others finally won him over. Before he left the Oratory he had changed completely. In time he rose to become a Minister of the Royal Household. When he returned to visit the Oratory, he told one of the Fathers that the example of Dominic on that particular occasion had done more for him than all the sermons he had ever heard since, either inside or outside the Oratory.

"Run off and tell Don Bosco!"

Do these words of young Ratazzi mean that Dominic Savio was sometimes a tattletale?

Fortunately, there is enough evidence to prove just the opposite. For instance, in this very incident with Ratazzi he was urged by the other boys to tell Don Bosco what had happened. They were on Dominic's side and they knew why he had not fought back. But Dominic did not breathe a word of it to Don Bosco, who learned all about it later from Ratazzi himself. Then there was the stone duel. Don Bosco learned about that, too, not from Dominic, but from one of the duelists.

Other important facts give some idea of how high Dominic rated on the campus. In a popularity contest conducted by Don Bosco, Dominic came out second. The winner was Rua, a clerical student at the time, much older than he and one of the "superiors" as well. It is easy to suppose that, if the contest had been limited to the younger boys, Dominic would have won.

It has already been mentioned, too, that Don Bosco said of Dominic: "He was well liked even by those boys who had no great love for their Faith."

Finally, one of the warmest friends that Dominic had, in life and in death, was John Cagliero, who is worth a whole book by himself. Dashing, vigorous, fiery, independent, straightforward, and loyal, he was far too noble to make a friend of anyone who could be mean.

In his early days at the Oratory, during the period of his friendship with Dominic, Cagliero was the despair of those in charge. Every day on his way back to the Oratory from school, though told time and time again not to break ranks, he insisted on running to the jugglers' booths in the Piazza. He would watch them closely, pick up a few new tricks, and then run all the way back to the Oratory. He could time it so well in the end, that he would catch up with the others just as they were entering the Oratory.

In a long story with a happy ending, both the amiable Dominic and the exuberant Cagliero ran into difficulty with the young cleric, Michael Rua, who was practically Don Bosco's right-hand man. Rua was a strict disciplinarian, first with himself and then with others. Once while he was teaching Dominic's class, Dominic burst out laughing and Rua checked him for causing a disturbance. A minute later Dominic burst out laughing again. One of the boys was doing something very amusing, but doing it only when Rua's back was turned. In the end the boy had Dominic laughing so much he could not stop. Rua decided to punish Dominic for his insubordination. He made him kneel down in the center of the classroom until class was over.

Rua was not impressed by the conduct of Cagliero. He even asked Don Bosco more than once to expel him. But each time Don Bosco appealed for a little more patience and "a few more drops of honey." He had in mind the day he was to invite all the seniors to become charter members of his new Society to look after boys.

The happy ending to the Rua-Savio-Cagliero story lies in the fact that all three became important figures in Don Bosco's Salesian Society and in the Church. Cagliero led the first band of Salesians ever to leave for the missions. He established the Salesians in South America, where they now hold a prominent position; he was the first of his Society ever to be consecrated bishop, and was eventually made a Cardinal by his great friend, Pope Benedict XV. Michael Rua was appointed the first successor to Don Bosco as Superior General of the Salesians, and, surprisingly enough, became famous not for the strictness of his ways, but for the fatherly kindness with which he treated all those with whom he came in contact. He died a holy death and his Cause for Canonization is making favorable progress.

Rua and Cagliero, as boys, were Dominic's intimate friends. Rua offered sworn testimony as to Dominic's sanctity; Cagliero, as Cardinal, was one of his stanchest supporters during the examination of the Cause for Dominic's Beatification.

CHAPTER 11

THE PLAGUE STRIKES

IN THE summer of 1854, a rumor was heard in Turin that sent a chill of horror into the hearts of the people, young and old, rich and poor. The dreaded cholera had reappeared in the South! This brought back to their minds the year of 1835, when 5000 had died in Naples within a few months. The wealthy sought refuge in the clear air of the hills but the disease followed them; those in the cities remained at the mercy of this hidden enemy, and all the precautions had so little effect that the people waited helplessly to see who would fall next.

Turin lived in dread that the disease would spread. At the end of July, it moved north and struck Genoa. Three thousand died within two months. Then, on August 7, it struck Turin, and the first victims dropped dead on the streets. After that, the city was in a nightmare. Deaths increased from ten, twenty, forty, to sixty a day; shops were closed and barricaded; people fled to the country; the streets were never without municipal death carts hurrying to the cemetery; mothers, suspecting that their children had been stricken, left them to die on the roads. The disease took its victims at all times and in all places; at home, in the street, with company, or alone. The symptoms were always the same: sudden violent pains in the intestines, cramps in the arms and legs; the flesh became livid and sometimes even blue, the eyesockets darkened, the whole appearance often changed so completely that the person became unrecognizable. The only difference was whether the victim died quickly or slowly. The sick writhed in pain and were picked up squirming on the sidewalks. Some died shortly after the attack, others lasted as long as twenty-four hours.

Medical science was helpless. In their ignorance, the people's fears multiplied. In the plague of Milan in 1630, they said the disease was spread by men who went about smearing poison ointment on church benches, walls, counters . . . anything that the people touched. This time in Turin they believed that the disease was being spread through the drinking water. The doctors were giving their patients poisoned water, said the whispers. They did this to get those who were beyond medical aid out of the way quickly.

The city hastily set up the only defense it knew. Huge infirmaries called *lazarettos* were opened into which all the victims of the plague were brought. They were given a treatment to combat the cold and cramps which followed the characteristic violent vomiting and diarrhea.

A newspaper article of the time praised the Oratory for its public spirit, and thanked Don Bosco for getting fourteen boys to volunteer as infirmarians at one time, and thirty more later when the city was desperately in need of help.

These volunteers went to work at the nearest *lazaretto*. They worked day and night, often going without their meals. Back at the Oratory, Mama Margaret emptied the house of all available clothing and linen. One day there was no more cloth in the house, so she went to the church, took an altar cloth, an amice, and an alb, and tore them up to make bandages.

Don Bosco fell victim to the disease, and so did Cagliero. Fearing to frighten the others, Don Bosco locked himself in his room, worked his body into a violent sweat, and fell asleep exhausted. He woke up the next morning completely cured. He told Cagliero not to worry because *his* time had not yet come, and there and then prophesied that John would travel far and one day be a bishop.

Among the families cared for by Dominic's companions was one in which a man, Moretta by name, came down with the disease. Before his illness, he had heard more than enough about the poisoned water. When he realized that he had cholera, the first thing he did while he still had his strength was to load a pistol and lay it beside his bed. Then he swore he'd shoot anyone not belonging to the family who attempted to come near him. Nobody, he said, was going to get *him* with poisoned water.

Partly to prepare her husband and partly to see if he could be persuaded to receive medical attention, his wife sent for a priest. The priest came to the house at once and opened the sickroom door. The patient took up the pistol in his shaking hands and pointed it at the visitor's head.

"I don't know if you're a priest at all," he said. "So I'll count three, then shoot. One . . . two . . ."

The visitor slipped out of the room and disappeared.

The cholera began its work, and in a matter of minutes the man's skin changed its natural red hue and became livid; his eyes lost their luster; he clutched at the bedclothes as spasms of pain seized him and twisted his body.

In despair, his wife sent for Don Bosco.

When Don Bosco arrived, he stood outside the sickroom door and called in.

"Moretta!"

"Who is it?" growled Moretta.

"It's me, Don Bosco. May I come in?"

"Come in, come in, Don Bosco. *You* certainly won't bring me any poisoned water."

Don Bosco entered the room, but he had barely crossed the doorway when the other stopped him.

"Wait!" said Moretta. "Show me your hands!"

Don Bosco showed him his right hand.

"The left hand! Show me the left hand, too!"

Don Bosco showed him his left hand.

"Now keep your arms down and shake your sleeves!"

Don Bosco kept his arms down and shook his sleeves.

"Now empty that bag you have and turn it upside down."

Don Bosco emptied the bag and turned it upside down.

"All right!" said the man, relieved. "Now I feel safer. Come over, Don Bosco, and hear my last confession."

Don Bosco went to the bedside, heard his confession, and prepared him for death. The sick man was placed on a stretcher carried by Dominic's friend, Tomatis, and another boy, and was taken to the infirmary where he died.

Another time one of the Oratory boys called Don Bosco in to administer the sacraments to a patient. Don Bosco told the patient that when he suffered an attack of intestinal pain, he should drink a little water for relief. The man thanked him for the advice and promised he would do so.

During the night the boy in attendance heard the patient complain of acute pains in the intestines. He ran up at once and poured out a glass of water.

"Here," he said to the patient. "It's time you drank some water."

The other gave him a wild look.

"What?" he cried, having completely forgotten Don Bosco's advice. "What did you say? It's time I drank that water?"

He leaped out of bed, staggered drunkenly across the room, and grabbed a shotgun he had left handy against the wall. He pointed it at the white-faced boy.

"Get out!" he screamed at the top of his voice, as he swayed on the floor of the room. "GET OUT!"

A year later, cholera struck again. This time it was brought by a soldier from Crimea where thousands had already died from it. Dominic was still too young to be among the senior boys, but he pleaded with Don Bosco and was allowed to accompany them as assistant infirmarian.

One day in October, 1855, as if moved by a sudden unexplained impulse, Dominic left the Oratory and made his way through a series of streets, alleyways, and lanes until he came to a certain house. He stopped and rang the bell.

A man appeared at the door.

"Well, son? Are you looking for someone?"

"Is there a woman here with the plague?"

"No, thanks be to God!" replied the man. "No one here with the plague."

Dominic stepped back a little. He re-examined the front of the house.

"And yet," he said half to himself, "and yet . . . there *must* be someone."

"My dear boy," said the man patiently, "I am sure you are mistaken. There are only three of us here, my wife, my brother, and myself. All three of us are well, thank God! Therefore . . ."

"No, no!" insisted Dominic. "It's here, all right. I am quite certain now. Won't you please look around to make sure there's no one here who needs our help?"

Touched by Dominic's appeal, the man declared he'd search the house from top to bottom if it would bring help to someone in distress.

After a brief search, they found the cause of the boy's agitation. In a little closet off the stairway, they came upon an old woman already breathing her last. She worked all day, it came out later, in a home for children, and at night, if she happened to finish too late, she sometimes slept in that warm closet without telling anyone. A priest was sent for immediately and the poor soul died in peace.

Another dramatic last-minute rescue of someone in trouble happened late one night, after Don Bosco had gone to bed.

He was awakened by an insistent knocking at his door.
"Don Bosco! Don Bosco!"

"Who's that?"

"Dominic, Father."

"What on earth do you want at this time of night?"

"Oh, please, Don Bosco! Can you come with me at once? Please!" said Dominic. "And bring all that you need to save a soul."

Because one was Dominic Savio and the other was Don Bosco, the priest dressed quickly, lit an oil lamp, and came down.

"Follow me, Father. This way," was all Dominic said.

"I hesitated before going," Don Bosco wrote afterward, "but he insisted, and since I had on other occasions proved the importance of these invitations, I agreed to go."

When eventually they reached the house, which Don Bosco could never find again, Dominic rushed up three flights of stairs and stopped before a door. A light still showed through the transom even at that late hour.

"In there," he said to Don Bosco. "They want you in there."

The door opened slowly to their knocking and a woman appeared. Her face was white and drawn.

"Oh!" she exclaimed when she saw who it was. "A priest! God bless you, Father! You're just in time!"

Don Bosco heard the story when he went into the dimly lighted room. The man had been a Catholic but had given up his Faith. Now, in his last moments, he wanted to become a Catholic again and die in the grace of God. After hearing the poor man's confession, the priest did his best to give him back his peace of mind. He had not long to do so, however, for the man died in his arms.

Talking about it later to some of the priests, Don Bosco said that, as far as he was concerned, half the miracle of that night lay in Dominic's amazing ability to find his way in and out of a maze of streets, in those days so dark that it was impossible to see even a number. Dominic twisted and turned like a hare in the hunt, with the priest hurrying at his heels so as not to lose sight of him and get lost. "Even in daylight," Don Bosco declared, "Dominic normally could never have found his way to that house or the road back to the Oratory. As for doing it in the dark . . ."

Dominic's efforts, of course, were not all confined to helping people die. They were often the means of helping them keep alive.

A city official of Turin who came from the same town as Dominic and had been at school with him under Father Cugliero, told Father Francesia that as a boy he ran away from home to come to Turin. After three days of aimless wandering the streets, he found himself homesick and hungry.

"Suddenly," he said, "Dominic appeared before me. It was a mystery how he could have known that I had even run away from home. 'Come along to the Oratory,' he said. 'You'll find it easy to pass the time there pleasantly.' I have always considered this a miracle, and as a sign of gratitude I intend to build a tomb for him."

Nor was this extraordinary gift limited to the city.

Once in September, 1856, out of a clear sky, Dominic went up to Don Bosco.

"Father," he said, "may I have permission to go home?"

"Why do you want to go, Dominic?"

"My mother is ill and our Lady wants me to cure her."

"Who told you she was ill? Did your people write to you?"

"Nobody wrote to me. I just know by myself."

After that the priest made no further inquiries, but gave the boy sufficient money to pay for the trip. Dominic left the Oratory saying he would be back very soon.

He traveled by coach to Castelnuovo and began to walk the few miles that remained before he reached home. About halfway along the road he met his father walking in the direction of Buttigliera where the doctor lived.

"Dominic!" Charles exclaimed, when he saw his son. "What in heaven's name are you doing here?" He was nervous and agitated.

"I'm going to see Mom, Dad. She's very sick."

"You go straight to your Granny's at Ranello." Dominic's father spoke to him sharply, and continued on his way to Buttigliera. Only afterward did he begin to wonder how Dominic had heard the news so soon.

Dominic kept on walking in the direction of Mondonio. When he came near home, several of the neighbors tried to stop him from going in to his mother but he insisted. When he entered the bedroom, his mother herself tried to get him to leave, because of the nature of her illness. She was expecting another baby and there were signs of serious complications.

"Darling," she pleaded, "go to one of the neighbor's houses. I'll call you when it's over."

Dominic heard nothing. Going up to the bedside, he

85 put his arms around his mother's neck and kissed her. Then he looked at her affectionately for a moment.

"Now," he said at last, "I can go back."

After his visit, he seemed to be anxious to return to Turin as soon as possible. He was fortunate enough to catch a late coach and that same evening reached the Oratory. He told Don Bosco simply that our Lady had cured his mother and then he went to bed.

Back in Mondonio, meanwhile, his father arrived with the doctor. When the doctor finished his examination he found there was nothing for him to do. The patient was already out of danger. Dominic's new little sister, Catherine, was born on September 10, without mishap, and Dominic's mother could only point to the little scapular with a green ribbon round her neck. Dominic, she explained, had hung it there when he had embraced her, and from that moment on she had felt no more pain.

The story of that little scapular did not end there. On his deathbed, Dominic remembered it and told his mother she must lend it to other women who were in pain. His sister, Therese, born two years after Dominic's death, testified at her brother's Cause that the scapular had passed from one house to another for years until someone forgot to return it and in that way it was lost.

CHAPTER 12

KING'S SECRET

THE saints are humble about their own great privileges. Don Bosco, when speaking of his visions, used to call them "dreams." Those who have read his life will remember how on one occasion he "dreamed" of Patagonia, and sent an account of all that he had seen in his dream to the Geographic Society of Lyon with no explanation. The Society awarded him a silver medal!

As Don Bosco had his "dreams," so Dominic had his "distractions."

"When I am at my prayers," he said, almost complainingly, "a distraction comes. Then I lose the thread of my thoughts and the hours fly past like minutes."

Don Bosco once made an attempt to question him on the origin and nature of these "distractions." For a moment or so the boy spoke very frankly and then as the questions became more intimate, he grew embarrassed. When the priest continued to probe deeper, the boy was so affected he burst into tears. After that interview, Don Bosco never again tried to plumb the depths of Dominic's "distractions." Dominic went through his years at the Oratory in humble simplicity, for Don Bosco made it his special concern to protect him from further embarrassment, and help him keep the secret of his "distractions."

There was, for example, the morning that Dominic failed to show up for breakfast. He was absent that day from classes, and missing at lunch. No one could imagine where he had gone.

Informed of this after lunch, Don Bosco thought for a moment. He said nothing, but made his way immediately to nearby St. Francis Church. Once there, he went to the rear of the altar. What he saw moved him deeply. Dominic was standing behind the altar, one foot almost on top of the other, his right hand holding on to the bookstand and his left hand on his chest. He was completely lost in contemplation.

Don Bosco watched him for a moment before he dared to speak.

"Dominic," he called out softly.

There was no response.

"Dominic," he called, louder than before.

Finally he took the boy by the arm and shook him gently.

Dominic seemed to come out of a trance. He looked around vacantly for a moment. Then he noticed Don Bosco.

"Oh," he said, "is Mass over already?"

"Dominic," said Don Bosco quietly, "it's now almost two o'clock."

The "distraction" had lasted seven hours!

Dominic looked confused, humbled, and completely at
a loss. Don Bosco, too, was beside himself with emotion,
but he carefully hid his feelings so as not to make Dominic
all the more confused.

"Go and have something to eat, my son," he said. "And
if anyone asks you what happened, tell them you were
doing something for me."

On another occasion, the priest was about to leave the
sacristy after Mass, when he heard Dominic's voice. On
entering the choir, he found his pupil once again in
ecstasy. This time, however, Dominic was speaking and,
as far as Don Bosco could judge, was receiving answers to
his questions.

"Yes, my God," Dominic was saying. "I have already
said so and I repeat it! — I love You and shall always do
so until I die. If You see that I might ever commit a sin,
please send me death before that happens. Yes, my God!
Death before sin!"

These were not all the visions Dominic had, Don Bosco
tells us, and perhaps they may not have been even the
most important ones. He once had a vision while standing
beside a companion; he went into ecstasy before the very
eyes of Don Bosco, when the latter began speaking to a
group of boys about the virtue of purity and its reward
in heaven. "These ecstasies came upon him," Don Bosco
wrote, "in various times and places: in the study hall,
going to and coming from class, even during class itself."

The most famous of all Dominic's "distractions," however, carried him beyond the frontiers of his native land,
and is called "The Vision of England."

Dominic could not have had much knowledge of what was happening around the world. But he certainly must have heard something about the revival of the Faith in England, if not from reading, then from listening to Don Bosco, who was always interested whenever anything of importance happened to the Church. Just at that time something was happening in England that was more important in Don Bosco's eyes than the arrival of the British in the Mediterranean with their new fleet, new colonial wealth, and new ideas called democracy.

John Henry Newman, the famous scholar, had begun the long and painful search for truth that was to lead him, in 1845, to the Catholic Church. Many other distinguished men of the University of Oxford were to come along with him. This was the cause of the revival of the Faith in "Mary's Dowry," which was a name for England before the time of King Henry VIII.

The Oxford Movement, as it was called, began as a movement by Anglicans to give a solid historical foundation to their Church. It ended in disillusionment for its leaders, the chief of whom was Newman. He and many of his companions were forced to admit that a true Church must exist, and if it did exist it must be the Catholic Church, with the successor of St. Peter at its head.

Both Dominic and Don Bosco were deeply interested in the conversion of England. Don Bosco prayed for England and made others do the same. A note in the diary of a young cleric at the Oratory named Bonetti reads: "Received Holy Communion this morning for England, according to the wishes of Don Bosco." Dominic, also, offered up Holy Communion for England. He even wanted to become a priest to be able, like the great Father Dominic Barberi of the Passionists, to go there to work for souls.

"How many souls," he said, "are awaiting our help in England! If I were strong enough and holy enough, I would go this instant and by preaching and good example try to win everybody back to God!" Cardinal Cagliero declared that Dominic's vision of England must have been the reward for his constant prayers for England's conversion.

On a morning of 1856, after receiving Holy Communion, Dominic fell into one of his "distractions," or visions of the future. Afterward he mentioned to Don Bosco that if ever he had an opportunity of seeing the Holy Father, he would have something to say that would console him.

"What would you tell the Holy Father?" asked Don Bosco.

"I would tell him," answered Dominic, "that in the midst of tribulations that await him, he still must not cease to think of England. God is preparing a great triumph for the Church in that country."

There are two prophecies contained in Dominic's words. One of them refers to the troubles that awaited Pius IX, of which we shall read later. As to the second prophecy, regarding the future of the Church in England, Dominic went on:

"I seemed to see a vast plain covered with people and over them hung a dense, gray cloud. The people were walking about in great numbers, but like men who did not know where they were going. A voice nearby announced:

Don Bosco and Dominic. From a painting by Grida.

Above and below: The house at Mondonio where
Dominic died, now a place for pilgrimages.

This is England. I was going to ask the person who said this some questions, when I saw the Holy Father, Pope Pius IX. Majestically dressed and holding aloft a brilliant torch, he advanced toward this great multitude. As the torch approached, the clouds rolled back until the people stood in a clear light as if it were now noon."

The following year Don Bosco went to Rome for the approbation of his Religious Congregation, the Salesians. By then he was so well liked by His Holiness he had no trouble being received in private. He told the Pope about Dominic's vision.

"This," exclaimed Pope Pius IX, "confirms me in my intention of working even more energetically than before for the return of England to the fold. And how hard I have already worked in that direction! What you have just told me is at least the good counsel of a pious soul . . . He must be a very privileged person."

Today the visitor to England can see how the Salesians there have always borne in mind Dominic's connection with their country. In the center of the grounds of their school at Oxford stands a statue of Dominic in white marble. It looks toward the village of Littlemore where from 1852 until 1854, in a low, gray stone building, Newman meditated on the path to Rome.

Speaking of these supernatural events after Dominic's death, Don Bosco told the Savio sisters that he had often sought advice from Dominic even on certain outside problems, and he had never once been wrong in taking it. He told some of those at the Oratory that he had collected many more similar facts about Dominic, but for the moment "he had been content to note them down, leaving it to others to publish them when it will be for the glory of God." Unfortunately these writings, like many others of Don Bosco, were lost. Cardinal Cagliero offers additional evidence that they once existed. "I know," he said, "that Don Bosco also left other records of certain extraordinary happenings regarding the boy which can no longer be found."

Dominic's swift rise to sanctity astonished those surrounding him who were competent to judge. For the others, Dominic continued to be a pleasant companion and good friend. Two of Dominic's schoolmates, Ballesio and Piano, were later questioned about his extraordinary gifts. Ballesio replied that he did not know anything about them; Piano, who had been a constant companion of Dominic on their walks to and from school, said, "I never saw anything extraordinary in Dominic's life."

Either these boys were very unobservant, or else Dominic was very careful to keep the King's secret to himself.

CHAPTER 13

SHINING ARMOR

THE whole structure of Dominic's sanctity was built around the virtue of the strong — purity. Even before he met Don Bosco — the tiger of purity — he had an instinctive love for it and a hatred for anything likely to spoil the innocence of his soul. That was why he and Don Bosco were immediately attracted to each other when the two first met at Becchi. Purity for both of them was not only a necessary condition for holiness; it was holiness itself. Don Bosco's system was based on it. Dominic's sanctity flowed from it.

Dominic had no illusions about the difficulties to be met with in keeping himself pure. He knew he would have to be constantly on guard to protect it. Despite the scoffers, he realized that purity was the virtue of the strong.

When Dominic came to Turin, the custody of his eyes was no easy matter for him. Once he confessed to Don Bosco that keeping his eyes under control in the city was such an effort that by the time he reached the Oratory he had a headache. In order to lessen temptation, he swore that he would never, any more than was absolutely necessary, look at persons of the other sex.

Don Bosco, who knew him more intimately than anyone else, says: "Those who admired Dominic's outward calm and self-control found it so natural to him that they might have been inclined to attribute this to the fact that he was made that way by his Creator. But those who understood him better, or who had charge of his education, knew that it was the result of his own great efforts assisted by the grace of God."

Many a time the boys, returning from the city, would ask Dominic's impression of something of note they had seen along the way.

"I'm sorry," Dominic would reply, "but I'm afraid I didn't see it."

"Oh, come off it, Savio!" they insisted. "What have you got eyes for, anyway?"

"I have eyes to look upon the face of the Mother of God, if and when I get to heaven."

Dominic had strength enough to give good example and courage enough to defend his beliefs openly and his influence soon made itself felt. It was not long before the boys in the Oratory and on the nearby streets would not dare to mention anything off-color in Dominic's presence.

One December evening in 1856, just before bedtime, he went with the rest of the boys to hear Don Bosco's thought on some incident of the day before sending them to bed. This evening the saint told them the story of St. Paul and the books.

We read in the life of St. Paul — Don Bosco began — of a very interesting thing that happened to him when he went to preach at Ephesus. God loved what Paul was doing, and began to work miracles for him. He worked so many miracles through Paul, that people would take towels and aprons that had touched Paul, and lay them on the sick. These objects cured people of their infirmities and freed them from possession by evil spirits.

Some of the magicians heard of this and thought they would try to do the same by using Paul's name.

"I command you to leave this man," said one false priest to a person possessed by the devil, "in the name of the Lord about whom Paul preaches."

But the evil spirit was ready for him.

"I know the Lord," he said, "and Paul I know, too. But who in the devil's name are you?"

Then the evil spirit left the man and, catching hold of two of these false priests, knocked their heads together, tore off their robes, and sent them away howling.

When the news of this got around, the other magicians and false priests were so scared they brought their books of magic for St. Paul to burn, although they had cost a considerable amount of money.

"Vaschetti," Don Bosco said to one of the boys when he had finished, "can you tell me why St. Paul preferred to *burn* the bad books at Ephesus, instead of selling them and giving the money to the poor?"

"Sure, Don Bosco," the boy answered. "St. Paul burned 'em because if he sold 'em they'd have been passed around and would have done harm to somebody else."

"Very good, Vaschetti! You got the point," said Don Bosco, and went on to talk to the boys about the evils of bad books.

Don Bosco's words gave Dominic an idea. He would do something to put a few bad books out of circulation. Unlike St. Paul, however, he would not travel to Ephesus or anywhere else. He would start nearer home.

His first opportunity came one afternoon as he was passing a seldom-used corner of the playground. A group of six boys, some of them bigger than himself, had gathered in a tight little circle, all six trying to read the same magazine at once. Occasionally one would glance over his shoulders, give a sharp look around, and then return to the magazine.

That glance told Dominic all was not well. They did not want anyone else to see what they were reading. Dominic got close enough to see that it was a slick magazine with glossy pictures. Some of the pictures were all right but some of them were all wrong.

"Just the kind of thing," Dominic thought, "that Don Bosco is trying to keep out of the Oratory!"

"Let's have a look," he said, and before the others could stop him he snatched the magazine out of their hands and tore it to pieces in front of them.

The biggest boy of the group went up to him.

"What did you do that for?" he asked, closing his fists.

"God didn't give you eyes to look at that garbage," answered Dominic fearlessly.

"We were only looking at the jokes."

"It wouldn't be much of a joke if you went to hell, would it?"

"We didn't see any harm in it."

"Worse for you. Your eyes must be getting used to the dirt."

Dominic could be a terror when aroused, and nothing aroused him more thoroughly than an attack on the standards of morality set by Don Bosco for the Oratory.

Once, on a Sunday afternoon, the boys from outside were enjoying the games with which the Oratory attracted youngsters to Catechism. There was no porter on duty at the gate, and a man slipped into the campus unobserved. He picked a spot behind one of the buildings, and using the props he carried in a small leather case, began to show the boys some tricks. Others were quickly attracted to the group and soon the man had around him a crowd of open-mouthed youngsters. Among them was Dominic, enjoying the show as much as anyone.

When the man saw that his tricks had captivated his young audience, he began to talk of things that were improper, guardedly at first, but then more openly when he saw that he was meeting with no opposition.

Dominic waited long enough to make sure of the man's intent. Then he strode up to him and with blazing eyes denounced him to his face. He turned to the boys.

"What's the matter with you, anyway?" he cried. "How can you stand there listening to these stories? Haven't you any sense? Let's get this man out of here!"

Dominic was returning from school one sweltering summer afternoon with a boy named John Zucca. It was a day when the hot, still air made even breathing difficult. When they came to a bridge, they stopped and sat down, letting their feet dangle over the waters of the Ruenta. Zucca threw straws into the river beneath and watched with idle interest as they floated past and disappeared under the bridge. Farther down he saw a group of boys playing on the riverbank, splashing in and out of the cool water.

"Oooof!" gasped Zucca. "Can't do anything on a day like this! Let's go for a swim!" He slithered down the grassy slope, and a moment later had plunged into the river.

Dominic followed him in.

On the way back home, Dominic was silent.

"Something wrong, Dominic?" asked Zucca, for Dominic was usually very cheerful company.

"I was just wondering," said Dominic, "if it was all right to go swimming there."

"Not right to go swimming? How come?"

"Well, the way some of the boys were talking and fooling around didn't seem right to me."

"Aw, Dominic! They didn't mean any harm."

A few days later the weather was just as hot and the two boys followed the same procedure — up to a point. When they left the bridge to go down to the water, Dominic balked.

"What's the matter, Dominic?" asked Zucca. "Aren't you going in?"

"No," said Dominic, "I don't think I'm too good at swimming."

"You don't have to be a swimmer to go for a dip."

"And if I started to sink?"

"Just do what we do and you can't go wrong."

"Well, anyway, I don't think it's right the way the boys were acting the other day."

"What they do isn't any of your business."

"I'll ask at home if they'll let me go swimming."

"Don't you dare do that! We'll all get in trouble if they know we're swimming here!"

"If that's how it is," Dominic said, "I'd rather not go in."

That first time, Dominic had received a shock at seeing how the boys acted while swimming. He saw the danger he was running into under such circumstances, and refused absolutely to join the boys in swimming again.

In his biography of Dominic, Don Bosco wrote that Dominic had refused to go swimming with the rest. This, of course, was perfectly true. Nevertheless, after Dominic's death, when the *Life* was published, Zucca insisted in the presence of the others that Don Bosco was wrong. Dominic had gone in for a swim. He, Zucca, had seen him do it.

The news spread quickly, and eventually reached the ears of Don Bosco. The saint gathered his facts and waited for the right moment to make them known.

The moment came one evening after supper when the boys were preparing to leave the dining room. There was a slight commotion near the door as they made way for Don Bosco. His visit at such a time meant something of importance. The saint walked up through the silent rows of boys to the front of the room and stood on a chair. His face was set, and without its usual smile.

"Something's up!" whispered the boys among themselves.

"It has come to my ears," Don Bosco began, "that someone has been placing doubt on what I have written about Dominic Savio. The part questioned is where I wrote that Dominic refused to accompany the rest of the boys who went into the river. That is perfectly true. He did refuse. Out of love of purity, I repeat, he did refuse. It is also true, however, that the first time he went in, he did so because he was urged to it by the very boy who began this whispering campaign. I deliberately omitted mention of the first incident because I wanted to hide, for his own sake, the name of the boy concerned. I thought he might have been grateful to me at least for sparing him this public shame."

Here he looked in the direction of Zucca, whose face had been reddening more and more while Don Bosco was speaking.

"Now, Zucca," he said, addressing the unfortunate boy, "you have only yourself to thank if tonight you feel ashamed — as indeed you have every reason to."

When Don Bosco left it was some time before anyone felt like breaking the silence. They had never heard Don Bosco speak so angrily before.

The mild-mannered and gentle saint showed his wrath that evening only because it was a question of defending modesty. Any attack on morality, subtle or open, slight or serious, was always vigorously repelled by the saint. On behalf of poor Zucca, the object of Don Bosco's wrath, it should be pointed out that later the saint declared that Zucca had been favored by our Lady with extraordinary graces.

Don Bosco was always very severe on the subject of

swimming without due regard for Christian modesty. On one occasion two of his boys played hooky to go swimming in the river Dora in Turin. On the riverbank, they received one of the warmest spankings of their lives from an invisible pair of hands.

They found out who the owner of those heavy hands was when the saint sent a letter from Lanzo, forty miles away, where he was staying at the time, to tell the Superior and the boys of the school what he had done. This incident, while amusing, is also illuminating. It shows how deeply the saint felt on the subject of modesty, the custodian of purity.

Taught by such a master, Dominic could not possibly have had an attitude toward purity other than the one so characteristic of him. About Dominic's purity, Saint Pius X once said to Cardinal Salotti, Postulator for the Cause: "A youth who has carried to his grave his baptismal innocence, who during the short years of his existence never revealed the presence of any defect, is really and truly a saint. What more can we expect?"

CHAPTER 14

THE LITTLE WAY

It is the will of God that all of us, without exception, should become saints. Besides, it is not too difficult to become a saint: the reward for even trying will be very great.

ONE Sunday evening of April, 1855, Dominic was present at a sermon Don Bosco gave to his boys. The above quotation was the substance of this sermon.

Dominic, now thirteen years old, listened carefully, and the sermon had a remarkable effect on him. It disturbed him so much that his habitual self-control for once deserted him. For a few days he grew silent, became unsociable, and lost his usual smile and cheerful ways. The boys soon noticed the change; so did Don Bosco, and he decided to question him.

"What's wrong with you these days, Dominic? Something unpleasant?"

"No, Don Bosco," answered Dominic. "Something pleasant!"

"What do you mean by that?"

With the complete confidence he always showed in Don Bosco, Dominic explained that he was suffering because his desire to become a saint had grown more intense. He was impatient, he said, with the slow progress he was making. He wanted to give himself up completely to the practice of severe penance and self-denial.

"Oh!" he exclaimed. "I feel a burning desire to become a saint! Please help me, Don Bosco! Only tell me what I have to do to become a saint!"

When Don Bosco's feast day, the Feast of St. John the Baptist, came round that year the saint told the boys that he would buy them the gifts they asked of him in writing. Next day Don Bosco found a note on his table from Dominic. As his gift, Dominic only wanted Don Bosco to help him become a saint.

At the end of the Retreat given that year, he approached a boy named Massaglia and asked him to become his secret monitor. Massaglia was to tell Dominic each week what faults he had observed in his conduct.

Massaglia, a sincere boy, doubted seriously that he should presume to find faults in Dominic, and said so.

"Listen, Massaglia," said Dominic, "suppose we leave the compliments aside and help each other to become saints. Are you game?"

Massaglia said he was, and the two formed a friendship that lasted until death broke it up.

Dominic was more fortunate than many in his confessor, for in Don Bosco he found an understanding soul who had not the slightest desire to chastise Dominic as young Saint Thérèse of the Child Jesus was later to be chastised for her "intemperate desires." On the contrary,

Don Bosco praised the boy for having such splendid aspirations. Observing, however, during one of their conversations about sanctity, that Dominic was actually trembling with emotion, the saint took him aside and spoke to him.

"Dominic," he said quietly, "you must, first of all, try to calm yourself. If you are disturbed, how can you possibly hear the voice of God? You must also exercise a constant but moderate cheerfulness. You must be persevering in the practice of your duties in church and in the classroom, and never omit taking part in recreation with your companions."

"But how on earth can I become a saint by being happy?"

"How on earth can you be sad, if you feel that our Lord is so near you?"

"And the games, Father?"

Don Bosco led him to a window that overlooked the playground.

"See that, Dominic? Down there your friends are having plenty of good fun. Your place is with them. That's your post of duty."

Although Dominic kept Don Bosco's instructions faithfully thereafter, in his thirst for suffering he managed to find hundreds of little ways to mortify himself. He walked slowly through the snow in order to feel the bite of the cold; he held his arms off the bench when kneeling in church; he kept his hands out of his pockets. . . .

They were all simple, easy, apparently unimportant things that he had learned either from the lips of his friend or from observation of the saint's practice. Don

Bosco called them "pious dodges" because they raised people by easy stages to the highest form of sanctity.

"I am not capable," Dominic told Don Bosco one day, as if summing up all that he had learned, "of doing great things, but I want to do everything, even the smallest things, for the greater glory of God."

Despite all the means that Dominic used to mortify himself, he never became a prey to melancholy. The adjectives that those around him constantly used to describe Dominic were "serene," "happy," and "good-humored." On his sickbed, he was the only one in the room to remain calm and cheerful, consoling his mother and telling his father not to worry.

Under the guidance of Don Bosco, Dominic began his swift ascension through the practice of "the little way," the simple way of sanctity later to be spread across the earth by St. Thérèse of the Child Jesus. It led to an apostolic life of the kind so necessary, according to the recent popes, in our own time. Pope Pius XI, who canonized the Little Flower, declared that he saw "in the spiritual type formed by Don Bosco in Dominic Savio, the exemplar of that life of Catholic Action of which the Church stands in such great need today."

The "little way" that Dominic adopted made saints out of characters so different as his own and that of Mickey Magone, the leader of a gang of dead-end kids; as that of the strait-laced Michael Rua and the fiery, outspoken John Cagliero. They were led along this way by Don Bosco to a sanctity that, in the words of Pope Pius XI, resulted from "the perfection of the ordinary."

First to discover some of the means Dominic used

to fight temptation was his mother. On making his bed, she found that he was in the habit of placing little pieces of wood, stones, or even thorny branches under him at night to disturb his rest. He continued to do this secretly when he came to the Oratory. Later he began to use the broken shells of nuts. These were even more painful and annoying, and if found, he reasoned, people would think he had just been eating nuts in bed.

In the winter he allowed chilblains to develop on his hands and feet. He even encouraged them by wetting them and then not drying them. When the chilblains did not develop of themselves, Dominic tried to start them. Monsignor Piano testified that he saw Dominic, on cold winter days, deliberately cut his hands with needles and pen nibs. When others, unknowing, expressed sympathy for what he must have been suffering, Dominic thanked them. "I find," he said, ambiguously, "that the bigger they are, the better it is for my health."

In the lives of some of the great saints it is recorded that after much temptation and suffering to keep their hearts pure, they were rewarded by God in a very singular manner: they were never allowed to be tempted again. St. Thomas Aquinas was one of these saints. According to tradition, two angels girded him with a cord one day to symbolize his liberation from temptation.

In Dominic's case, Father Rua and others asserted that his mortifications, practiced as a safeguard, eventually earned for him complete freedom from temptations against the angelic virtue. Dominic, however, had first proved, by his conduct, that he was prepared to go through any trial rather than offend.

Despite all this, it still seemed to Dominic that he was not doing enough. Urged by a strange, unexplained feeling of being pressed for time, he decided to step up his mortification schedule. He decided that he could cover the road to sanctity in less time, if he used fasting as a short cut.

"Don Bosco," he said one day, "may I start fasting on bread and water every Saturday in honor of our Lady?"

"No."

"Well then," Dominic persisted, "may I wear a hair shirt sometimes to do a little penance?"

"No."

Dominic then confessed that he had already been doing a little extra fasting "just for Lent." Don Bosco stopped this, too. Then he gave the boy a lesson in sanctity that was as sound as it was homely: Dominic was to keep with all his might the ordinary rules of the school; he was to suffer the heat and cold of the day, the occasional pangs of hunger and thirst, sickness — just as God sent them and because they came from Him. If he did that, he could not help but become a saint.

Soon after this there was another encounter between Dominic, intent on finding ways of becoming a saint faster, and Don Bosco, equally intent on moderating his zeal and guiding it into the proper channels.

In the bitter cold month of January, 1856, Dominic caught a chill and was ordered to bed. On making his customary rounds of the house, Don Bosco came upon him and, of course, asked him how he felt. But while talking to the boy, he saw something that caused him to stare in horror.

"Do you mean to tell me," he exclaimed, "that you are using only one thin sheet to cover yourself in this cold room? Do you want to die of pneumonia?"

"No, Father," replied the boy, "I thought that when our Lord was on the cross, He had even less to cover His poor body."

That did it! In no uncertain terms, Don Bosco forbade Dominic from then on to undertake any penances, big or small, long or short, unless he had express permission.

"But, Father," Dominic complained, "our Lord says that if we want to go to heaven, we have to do penance. If I am not allowed to do any penance, how can I get to heaven?"

"The penance that our Lord wants from you is obedience. Obey, that's all."

"And you won't allow me to do any penance at all?"

"Yes; I'll allow you to suffer patiently any insult or injury that may come your way. I have already told you I'll allow you to suffer with resignation the heat, the cold, the rain, sickness, fatigue, and all the other ills that God will be pleased to send you."

"But, Father," insisted Dominic, "those are things I can't avoid anyway!"

"That's right. But if you just offer up everything, it will become an act of virtue and you'll gain merit by it. Now, I'm going to send up some blankets to keep you warm. If I find you without them when I come round again — may the Lord have mercy on you!"

Don Bosco's sermon on becoming a saint inspired Dominic so much that it marked for him another step along the road to sanctity.

CHAPTER 15

THE IMPERIAL GUARD

GOD was in a hurry with Dominic. He had to make him a complete work of divine art, a perfect model, within a short span of life. On his part, Dominic had an inner awareness of God's design, or at least of his limited time on earth. He was often heard to say: "I have to hurry to become a saint, before it is too late."

The year 1856 was one of great activity for him. He felt the urge again to do something out of the ordinary for our Lady and, with the approach of the month of May, he decided that the time had come. "I must do something special in honor of the Mother of God, but" — again that sense of haste — "I'll have to hurry, for I'm afraid there won't be much time."

He and a few friends decided to decorate our Lady's altar in the dormitory in a way that would be long remembered. They agreed to buy some flowers and fancy cloth for decorations. Everybody put something into the fund. Everybody, that is, except Dominic. Dominic did not have a penny to his name, because whatever little money he had, he always gave it to Don Bosco for some good cause.

Without explaining why he had no money to put up, he went to his boxes and took out all the books he had won as prizes. Some of the others contributed a few articles and chances were printed and sold among the boys at a fair profit. Dominic deposited the entire amount with the group, as his contribution to our Lady's altar.

But neither this nor the hundred other little things that Dominic did privately to honor our Blessed Lady really measured up to what he had in mind. It would have to be, he said, something very special. What that "something special" was, and how it came to be realized, makes an interesting story.

Don Bosco always interpreted the laws restricting Holy Communion very broadly for his time. He refused, for instance, to follow the common practice of having his boys go to Confession and Communion bench by bench and row by row. At the Oratory, he allowed far greater freedom than would have been tolerated elsewhere. He always encouraged the boys to receive Holy Communion as often as their confessor would allow.

One morning, therefore, in May, 1856, when Don Bosco was saying Mass for the boys, he turned around at Communion time and held up the Host for adoration; then he looked down to see how many boys were going to receive. There was not one at the altar rail. A morning in the month of Mary, and neither Cagliero nor Rua — not even Dominic himself — at the altar rail! Don Bosco was so visibly upset that many of the boys noticed it.

One of these was a boy named Durando. Celestine Durando had come to the Oratory in the spring of 1856, and had brought with him a love of study and a hatred of priests. Personal contact and a little understanding proved to be the gradual and simple means of changing his heart. His hate turned into affection, and he became so attached to priests in general that he ended up by becoming one himself! On this occasion the idea was born in his mind of forming a group which would make sure that Don Bosco would not be disappointed like this again. One day, on the way to Professor Bonzanino's school, he mentioned this idea to Dominic, and found him enthusiastic. They gathered a few friends together and formed a Communion Club. Dominic and Durando had the members choose days for receiving Holy Communion in such a way that the altar rail would never again be empty at Communion time.

Not long after its foundation, the Communion Club burst into a blaze of glory. Dominic, who at these club meetings was said to talk "like a little Doctor of the Church," knew that Don Bosco wanted them to set a date for a general Communion. He suggested to the others that they choose Christmas Eve. The boys accepted this date with enthusiasm and began a drive to boost the Club's intention.

Christmas Eve of 1856 came, and Don Bosco celebrated the Midnight Mass. At Communion time, he turned around hopefully. His eyes lit up. Not only was the altar rail full, but the whole church was crowded with boys, boarders and day boys, all waiting to receive! It was a wonderful triumph for the Communion Club. Once

again Don Bosco was visibly moved when he looked at
the altar rail, but this time for a very different reason.
He had to wait to compose himself before he could go
on with the Mass.

Dominic had been quick to see certain possibilities in
the Communion Club. He first spoke of his idea to Don
Bosco who gave it full approval, then he approached a
few boys who he thought might be interested. They were.
The next day Dominic and his friends launched their new
idea: a Sodality of the Immaculate Conception. On Sunday, June 8, 1856, about a dozen boys, including Savio,
Rua, Cagliero, and Durando, were professed as members
of the new Sodality.

The boys appointed a committee to draw up a set of
rules, and undertook to enlarge their program from the
reception of Holy Communion to include any other
activities that would safeguard morals in the school.

Don Bosco examined the rules they formulated:
— Observe the Rules of the House.
— Occupy one's time well.
— Tell one another of defects.
— Receive Holy Communion frequently.
— Recite the Rosary daily.
— Be satisfied with the regular food.

"Good," was Don Bosco's comment. "I won't make any
changes. But I want you to understand, of course, that
these rules do not bind even under pain of venial sin.
Also, better not add any more religious practices without
first consulting me."

Since the day of its birth, the Sodality never looked
back. It spread all over the world, and today does immense

good in hundreds of schools and colleges, and, among other things, provides thousands of vocations to the priesthood and religious life.

One of the more interesting tasks that Don Bosco entrusted to Dominic and his associates of the Sodality was that of "adopting" a boy at the Oratory. When the number of boys living at the Oratory increased to around 170, Don Bosco did not have time to give everyone individual supervision and care. Yet he knew that a few boys had come to the Oratory after having led questionable lives outside. The Sodality, therefore, "adopted" a boy chosen by Don Bosco, and made special efforts to bring him around to a better kind of life.

New boys, too, were a particular care of the Sodality. Dominic insisted on this. Even long before the Sodality was founded he used to go out of his way to help new boys find their feet.

Frank Cerrutti, afterward famous as the compiler of a popular Italian dictionary, in giving evidence at Dominic's Cause, told how clever Dominic was in making new boys feel at home.

In Frank's case Dominic had a talk with him, and learned from his conversation that he was good at words. He asked him to explain "somnambulist." Frank launched into a careful explanation: *Somnum* means sleep, and *ambulare* means to walk; so we get "somnambulist" — "sleep" and "walk" — "sleepwalk." From that day on, Frank liked the Oratory and grew to love it so much that he, like Durando, stayed there as a boy — priest — professor — for over 70 years!

Camillus Gavio was a quiet boy of brilliant intellect.

He had a talent for painting and sculpture, and had just won a municipal scholarship. He had come to the Oratory convalescing from a serious illness. Dominic met him wandering around aimlessly, after the manner of the sick, and looking at everything with lack-luster eyes.

"Hello," said Dominic. "You don't know anybody yet, I suppose?"

"No, not yet," replied Camillus, "but I enjoy watching the boys play games."

"What's your name?"

"Camillus Gavio of Tortona."

"How old are you?"

"Fifteen."

"What makes you so sad looking? Are you sick?"

"Yes, I was very sick. I had palpitation of the heart, you know. And I was nearly dying. I'm not cured yet."

"Don't you want to get cured?"

"Not so much," was the surprising answer. "I just want to do the will of God."

Dominic looked at him.

"If you want to do the will of God," he said, "you must want to become a saint. *Do* you want to become a saint?"

"What do I have to do?"

"Well," said Dominic, echoing Don Bosco's words, "you know that in the Oratory we become saints by being very cheerful about it; we try our best not to commit any sins, big or small; we study and play and follow the practices of piety. Don Bosco always tells us to serve God with a smile."

Camillus had not much longer to serve God. He died two months after that meeting on the day Don Bosco had foretold. Dominic, who had assisted him during his final illness, was not allowed, despite his appeals, to stay in the sickroom during the night, and Camillus died in the presence of Don Bosco.

Many other sodalities branched off from the original. One of these was the Altar Boys Sodality. This was such a novelty at the time that thousands were attracted to the Oratory to see what they found difficult to believe: little boys, no higher than one's elbow, dressed like small dignitaries, serving High Mass with respect and gravity. In the choir loft their companions sang the difficult Gregorian music of the Mass.

Another group that had its roots in the Sodality, was the Society of the *Tocc.** These boys were, perhaps, a little more advanced than the others in the spiritual life. They sought to mortify themselves by gathering up the *tocc* or pieces of bread from the table and the floor so that they would not be wasted. Frank Cerrutti testified that he saw Dominic gather up the crusts of bread and ends of cheese the others had thrown away and make a meal out of them, refusing, in the meantime, his regular supper portion.

From the ranks of the Sodality of the Immaculate Conception and its branch associations came those who were to be the charter members of the future Congregation, the Salesians. From them also Don Bosco recruited what he called his "Imperial Guard" and upon which he leaned heavily for assistance in running the Oratory.

The Imperial Guard was a select and distinguished

---

* *Tocc* (pronounced "touch") is a word in Piedmontese corresponding to the Italian *tozzo,* meaning a piece or morsel.

corps to which it was considered an honor to belong. It differed from the Sodality in its manner of dealing with other boys. Where the Sodalists "adopted" a boy secretly, the Imperial Guard worked clearly in the open. The whole Oratory knew that the Imperial Guard stood squarely on the side of law and order.

Thus from the small beginning of the Sodality many other groups branched out and worked hand-in-hand for the success of the Oratory. These groups, forerunners of our modern Catholic Action, have long since spread beyond the limits of the Oratory, through thousands of schools and youth organizations, and still keep increasing rapidly in numbers.

In this way, Dominic achieved his wish to do "something special" for our Lady before, as he said, it was too late.

When questioned about Dominic and the Sodality, Father Rua said: "I always admired the heroic way he practiced his religion during his stay at the Oratory. But my growing admiration increased a thousandfold after the foundation of the Sodality of the Immaculate Conception."

This was the fourth and last step that Dominic took along the road to sanctity.

CHAPTER 16

HOMEWARD BOUND

"I'm AFRAID you'll have to leave the Oratory, Dominic," said Don Bosco.

"Gee, Father! You don't really mean that, do you?"

"I'm sorry, Dominic, but that's how it is. You'll have to leave."

Dominic walked away with his head down. For him this was the bitterest moment he had experienced since the day he met Don Bosco. Walking across the playground he recalled the happy time he had spent at the Oratory; the fun and games, the picnics, the stage with its plays and skits, the chapel with its ceremonies and choir, and, of course, the pleasant feeling he had when Don Bosco was around.

Now he was being asked by Don Bosco himself to leave the Oratory. Worse than that, he was convinced that he would never be allowed to return.

What had happened within the past few months to force Don Bosco to send him away?

117

Aware of certain symptoms of the boy's failing condition, Don Bosco decided to keep a more watchful eye on Dominic's health. For one thing he felt that the long journey to school outside the Oratory was too much for the boy and he ordered him to stay home. As a substitute for the outside schooling, he arranged for Dominic to have private lessons from Father Francesia, who was then beginning the first classes at the Oratory.

Once the outside classes stopped, Dominic's health improved, and he gained weight during the spring and early summer of 1856. The improvement was not permanent, however, and he again began to fail. This time Don Bosco called in a specialist and friend, Dr. Vallauri, to make a thorough examination. The verdict was not reassuring. Savio would have to be very careful, the doctor warned, so save what little strength he had left.

Dominic received this serious news calmly. More concerned with the health of his soul than with that of his body, he asked the saint how he might make the month of May an especially good one. From Don Bosco he received three recommendations: Do his ordinary duties well, receive Holy Communion with good dispositions, and tell someone a little story every day about the Mother of God.

"I'll do that, Father," he said, "Now what grace do you think I should ask for?"

"Ask her to obtain good health for you . . . and the grace to become a saint."

Dominic took Don Bosco's three recommendations to heart. To do his ordinary duties well had always been one of the main points of his conduct. To receive Holy

Communion with good dispositions was not difficult for
him. When allowed to receive only once a week, like
St. Aloysius Gonzaga he had divided the week into two
parts; the first he used in preparing for Holy Communion,
the second in thanksgiving for having received. During
his second year at the Oratory, Don Bosco had allowed
him to receive Communion daily, although daily Communion, as a common practice, was not introduced into the
Oratory until 1878. As to telling someone each day a little
story of our Lady, he started that right away.

And right away he ran into rough water. The first time
he began to tell a story to a group of boys, one of them
objected.

"Why do you bother about these things?" the boy said
impatiently.

Dominic flared up immediately.

"Why do I bother?" he repeated with indignation. "I
bother because the souls of my companions were paid for
with our Lord's life; I bother because as buddies we
should be helping one another; I bother because God
says we should save souls. If we save the soul of another,
we save our own as well! — That's why I bother with
these things!"

Soon after this, Dominic grew too ill to go to class and
was confined to the sickroom. He passed the time attending to the wants of the other patients. He had his own
way of entertaining them. He kept them interested with
talks on death!

"This old carcass of ours can't possibly last forever,"
he said as an introduction. Then he launched into his

subject enthusiastically. "But when we die our souls are freed; all our chains fall off; then our bodies fly to heaven as well, and enjoy a health that lasts forever and ever! — Meanwhile, my friend," he added wryly, as he brought a dose of medicine to his listener, "you must take this awful stuff they sent you, for God made medicine to help us get well again, if possible."

Despite his failing strength, Dominic insisted on sweeping the floors, dusting the furniture, bringing up the food, cleaning and polishing the boys' shoes.

"I like to do this for them," he replied to those who protested. "It's such a pastime for me I'm sure I get no merit for it."

His condition grew steadily worse and Don Bosco became more and more concerned. Finally he decided to invite several doctors in for a consultation. Dr. Vallauri was present. During the minute examination that followed, Dominic showed no signs of being disturbed. When the consultation was over, it was Dr. Vallauri who brought the second verdict: there was very little hope that the boy would ever get better.

In private, the doctor had a verdict of another kind to give Don Bosco. "What a precious pearl you have in that boy, Don Bosco!" he said.

"I know it, Doctor," said Don Bosco. "But what would you say was the origin of this sickness, this wasting away?"

"I would say with deep conviction, Father, that the rather delicate health, the intelligent spirit, the tension — all these certainly have been wearing down his strength."

"And the remedy?"

"The remedy? My dear Father, let him go to heaven. He is ready. Meanwhile to lengthen his short span of life somewhat, he should be relieved at once of all mental strain. Take him away from studies and put him to some kind of light, manual work."

A short while before this illness, Dominic received a letter from his intimate friend, Massaglia, who was then at home.

My dear friend,

I thought I was leaving the Oratory for only a few days, but now it seems that it will be for a long, long time. The state of my health is more uncertain every day. The doctor says I am getting better, I say I am getting worse. We shall soon see who is right.

How sorry I am to be away from you and the Oratory! My only comfort is the thought of the days we used to set aside to receive Holy Communion together.

Will you please go to my place in the study hall? You will find there my *Imitation of Christ*. Make a small parcel of this and send it to me.

Keep smiling! If we cannot stay longer together in this life, I hope we shall live together in heaven.

Affectionately yours,
JOHN MASSAGLIA

Dominic answered his friend's letter:

My dear Massaglia,

I was glad to hear from you. It was a sign that at least you are still alive. We did not know whether to say "Glory be to the Father!" or "Out of the Depths"!

You must remember that Thomas à Kempis is a long time dead and never budges in his grave. It is up to you to make him live again by trying to put into practice what he says.

You tell me that you are not sure if you will ever come back to the Oratory. My own old carcass seems to be used up, and everything warns me that I am quickly coming to the end of my life. Whatever happens, let us pray for each other that we may both have a good death. Whoever reaches heaven first can prepare a place for his friend, so that when the other goes, he will find someone waiting there to welcome him.

Affectionately yours,
DOMINIC SAVIO

Massaglia never returned to the Oratory. He died on May 20, 1856, a few days after receiving the letter from his friend. Did Dominic know that his letter was to be a warning to Massaglia?

The news of his friend's death had a curious, saddening effect on Dominic. For the first time, writes Don Bosco, he saw the boy fall into a state of depression. Perhaps it was because Massaglia had been Dominic's best friend at the Oratory, and this untimely death made him feel the pain of loss more keenly. It also brought closer to him the thought of his own end.

The summer vacation of 1856 was a godsend for Dominic's health, and every day he spent at home brought some improvement. Following his custom, Don Bosco paid his annual visit to his own home at Becchi, this time accompanied by Rua. He received an agreeable surprise. Believing his pupil to be still in bed, he sent Rua to visit him. Rua met Dominic walking along the country lanes, round-cheeked and full of spirit. Shortly after this meeting, he was taken out of the hands of the doctor and in the fall he returned to the Oratory to recommence outside classes under Professor Picco.

In the foreground: The three people whose cures were considered in Dominic's canonization (see Chapter 20).

Dominic's picture, carried in procession during the canonization ceremonies in Rome.

The winter of 1856 was an extremely severe one in Turin — the coldest winter, in fact, within the memory of the living. It was also a sad one for the people of Piedmont, for the unhappy outcome of the Crimean War had thrown them into a disastrous state of even greater poverty and suffering. At the Oratory, too, there was an added touch of misfortune. Don Bosco's mother, Mama Margaret, an angel of love to all the boys, was brought down with a dangerous attack of pneumonia. Despite the prayers of the boys and the best of medical care, she died on November 25.

Once Dominic was back in the routine of studies and life at the Oratory, his health again began to decline. He gradually weakened, and developed a painful cough besides. Now his disposition seemed to change. He became rather unsociable, and seemed to avoid his companions. The change was so noticeable that Joey Cheano, one of his friends in the Sodality, mentioned it to him.

"Don't you like to talk to your friends any more, Dom?" Joey asked.

"Oh, yes!" Dominic exclaimed, his brows gathered up in pain. "It isn't that. It's only because when I speak at all, I feel two knives cut right through both my temples!"

Severe stomach pains now forced him to eat less and less. He always accepted the food that was served to everyone and consistently refused to ask for, or even to accept, anything special at table.

At last, for the boy's sake, Don Bosco had to make the unpleasant decision of sending him home again. Since Dominic was showing no signs of improvement at the

Oratory, perhaps he might recover back home in his native air. He had done so before. It was, therefore, suggested to him gently that he should return to Mondonio.

"I'm sorry, Dominic," was what Don Bosco had to tell the boy, "but it would be better for you to go home for another rest. Put your books aside for a while, and stay outdoors as much as possible. When you have recovered you will be very welcome back at the Oratory."

"No, no," sighed Dominic. "This time, if I go, it will be to return no more."

Wondering at the boy's strange unwillingness, Don Bosco asked, "But why don't you want to go home?"

"Because I want to die at the Oratory," said Dominic.

On the eve of his departure, Saturday, February 28, 1857, Dominic was present with the rest of the boys at the practice known as "The Exercise of a Happy Death." When it came to the part where prayers are said "for the one among us who will be the first to die," those near Dominic heard him say "for *Dominic Savio* who will be the first to die."

Next morning after Mass he stopped one of the boys and handed him a small sum of money that he had borrowed.

"Here," he said. "Let's get our accounts settled. I don't want to be embarrassed with debts in front of our Lord."

The next day was a sad one for Dominic. Don Bosco and all those who knew him were not too happy either. Intent on receiving a final word from his guide and friend, Dominic went up to the saint.

"What can a sick person best do to get to heaven, Father?"

"Offer up to God all you have to suffer."

"Anything more?"

"Offer your life to Him."

Dominic seemed satisfied for a moment. But he grew doubtful again.

"Can I be certain all my sins have been forgiven?" he asked.

"I assure you, in God's name, that your sins have already been forgiven."

"How about when the devil comes to tempt me?"

"Tell him that you've sold your soul to God. If he still makes trouble, ask him what *he* ever did for you, compared to what Christ did."

"Will I be able to see the Oratory from heaven — and Mom and Dad?"

"Yes, you'll see what's going on at the Oratory. You'll see your mother and father. You'll see a thousand beautiful things besides."

"Will I be able to visit them, do you think?"

"Yes, you will, if that is for the greater glory of God."

Only Dominic seemed convinced that his death was just a few days away. Therefore, his departure from the Oratory, had a very special meaning for him, since he alone was certain that he was leaving it for the last time. When his father arrived to take him home, he grew downcast.

"So you don't want to keep this old carcass any more, Father," he complained. "I guess it wouldn't be for much longer. Anyway, God's will be done!"

Don Bosco protested that he would have given worlds to keep him at the Oratory, but the doctors had said he must go back to his native air in the hope that it might save his life. Don Bosco felt it was his duty to send him home.

Dominic made one last request before he said good-by. "Father, I should like a little present before I go."

"I'll give you anything you wish. What is it? A book?"

"Something better than that."

"Money for the journey?"

"Right!" exclaimed Dominic. "That's it! Money for the journey to heaven! You said something about having some special indulgences for the dying. Will you put my name down for them?"

"Certainly, Dominic! I'll put your name in the book at once."

"Good-by, Don Bosco!" said Dominic and he kissed the priest's hand.

"Good-by, Dominic!"

"As I chatted with him," said Cagliero, who was among the group of boys seeing him off, "I saw him wear that same old smile. Knowing what it was costing him to leave us, I said to myself, What a great little saint he must be!"

CHAPTER 17

NEW ADVENTURE

"MOTHER, I have something important to tell you," said Dominic as soon as he reached home.

"What is it, dear?"

"I know I'm going to frighten you and Dad, but I must tell you that I'm going to die soon."

Bridgit Savio was startled. Raimonda stopped halfway across the kitchen. Charles Savio, not knowing what to do, rubbed his hands together and kept darting glances from one to the other.

"What! Going to die soon?" echoed his mother. "For the love of God, dear child, don't say things like that!"

"But it's true, Mother," insisted Dominic.

"Come on up to the attic, son," said his father at last. "We got it ready again when we heard you were coming back. You've been traveling all day and you need a rest."

Dominic followed his father up the narrow stairs. Charles and Raimonda puttered about his room for a moment or two, adjusting and rearranging. Finally they left him. Dominic lay on his bed and heard all the faint familiar noises of the countryside come up to him. Downstairs they were discussing something in low tones. He listened vaguely for a while until the voices melted away and he fell asleep.

Charles and his wife were talking in the kitchen.

"You don't think there's anything in what he said, do you, Charles?" asked Bridgit.

"Not by the looks of him tonight, anyway," said Charles.

"He looked wonderful to me," said Bridgit. "His face is redder than mine. And yet Don Bosco wrote . . ."

"It was so red," put in Raimonda, "I thought he'd been drinking wine."

"I wonder what put such notions into his head?" said Bridgit.

"I suppose because he saw Massaglia and one or two of the others die, he imagines he'll go, too," said Charles.

"Yes, yes," said Bridgit. "That's the reason."

She went into the kitchen and returned with two eggs in her hand. Before she broke the eggs she turned again to her husband.

"Maybe, after all," she said, "we should call in the doctor — not that there's anything — but just to quiet him."

"It won't do any harm," Charles agreed.

On Wednesday of that week Dr. Cafasso came to examine Dominic. He thought Dominic's condition grave enough when he diagnosed it as inflammation of the lungs. (This was the medical term of those days for pneumonia.) He himself would come up on the following day to try the effect of bloodletting.

Curing ailments by draining off the patient's blood was

widely practiced in those days. Its success, as can easily be imagined, was highly uncertain. Nevertheless, it was the established practice and Dr. Cafasso acted in accordance with tradition, when he tried a "little bleeding," as he called it, on his patient. He should have hesitated, though, especially since he had to try it ten times within the space of four days.

The first time he came for the treatment, he laid out his instruments in a neat row on the little bedside table.

"Now, sonny," he said cheerily, "everything is going to be wonderful. No need to be afraid. Only, I don't want you to look. You might get frightened, you know. Turn round now. There's a good soldier!"

"You needn't worry about me, Doctor," said Dominic calmly. "I don't think I'll get frightened."

"No, no!" said the doctor firmly. "They all say that and then when the knife — then they spill blood all over the place."

"But what's a little knife like that," said Dominic, "compared to the nails that went right through the hands and feet of our Lord?"

The scalpel stopped on its downward journey. The doctor stared. But only for an instant, and then he gave his whole attention to the operation. With a slight jerk of the wrist, he sank the point of the blade into the patient's arm . . .

"Quite a saint, that boy," was his terse comment outside. From that moment on, he began to look upon Dominic with different eyes.

After the bloodletting the doctor's verdict was encouraging. Nothing to worry about, he said. The patient would soon be right as rain. A little weak, perhaps, but his mother could easily build him up again with extra food.

"Good kitchen air and wine-cellar soup." He smiled as he quoted an old Italian remedy.

Once the news of Dominic's illness spread, a surprising number of friends and neighbors in the area came to visit him. Dominic was well known to them. They were as fond of him as their children were, and they brought gifts, little and large, of fruits, food, and wine. The generous gifts of those who could afford them Dominic passed to poorer people. As each visitor left, Dominic called out: "See you again — in heaven!"

"Eat the nuts and then bring back the shells," he told them. "I'm saving 'em up."

With all this care and attention, his appearance began to improve. He looked healthier and stronger than before and his cheeks took on a little color. His parents were pleased, the neighbors were pleased, and, most of all, the doctor himself was pleased. Charles asked his son what *he* thought.

"I think it is now time," he said, "to receive Viaticum before I die."

The calm way he said it and the apparent inappropriateness of the remark made his parents doubt for a moment that he was in his right mind.

"Let's not be taken unawares," Dominic replied to all objections. "Better receive the Sacraments too early than too late."

Only after long insistence on Dominic's part did they agree to call the pastor. He came and administered the last rites to the boy, who, when it was all over, felt quieted. What seemed to cause him his greatest anxiety was the thought that he was giving so much trouble.

"I don't want to be a bother to my folks," he said. "They've had enough worry over me. I only wish there were some way to repay them."

Next day the doctor arrived for his morning visit, unaware of what had happened the day before. Nor did the parents have the courage to inform him. They were afraid of what the doctor might say to them for not trusting his diagnosis.

"We've beaten the sickness, my boy!" the doctor said breezily. "All we have to do now is to take it nice and easy."

"We've beaten the world, Doctor," was Dominic's reply. "All we have to do now is prepare to appear before God."

It was now the doctor's turn to doubt the boy's sanity. He left the house in an anxious frame of mind.

Dominic began to count the days and the hours with almost mathematical precision. Yet through it all he never for a moment lost his old lightheartedness.

Two days later, at noon on March 9, he had a relapse. Bloodletting had sapped the last ounce of strength from his frail body, and left him no reserve vitality with which to combat any further attacks.

The pastor was called in, urgently this time. He administered Confession and Communion and gave the patient the Papal Blessing for the dying.

"The Holy Father sends his blessing, Dominic," said the pastor.

"Thanks be to God! Thanks be to God!" was all the sick boy said.

While the pastor was still at the house, the boy recovered greatly and returned almost to normal. Under the circumstances, the priest felt embarrassed at suggesting thoughts for the dying to one who seemed so very much alive.

"Can't you give me a little thought to meditate on?" the patient pleaded.

"Think of the Passion of our Lord," said the pastor. Dominic went off into a doze, and the pastor left the house saying he would be back if things took a more serious turn.

Dominic's father and mother, also, felt somewhat confused because there had been so many unexpected elements in the little drama. Now they could only wait. Bridgit left the sickroom to attend to her household chores, and Charles kept watch by the bedside. After a long and tiring vigil, he saw the sick boy stir.

"It's coming now, Dad," whispered Dominic.

"Eh, son? . . . Do you want something?"

"Time's up, Dad," said the boy quietly and distinctly. "Please get my prayer book and read for me the Prayers for a Happy Death."

Charles Savio took up the little book of prayers Don Bosco had written for his boys. It included some prayers for the dying. His voice faltered, perhaps because he met an unfamiliar word, perhaps because he was overcome at the thought of his approaching loss. Each time his son answered the prayers, it brought back to him the memory of how they used to sing the psalms together at the smithy. Now they were saying the prayers for the dying together. Sometimes God's will was very hard to accept.

As they neared the end of the prayers, Dominic's mother came running in. One glance was enough. She understood at once and fell down on her knees, covering her face with her hands.

"Surely you're not crying, Mom," said Dominic, "at seeing me go to heaven!"

Strangely enough, after this show of concern for his mother, Dominic seemed unaffected by his immediate surroundings. He no longer responded to his father's inquiries, nor did he look at his mother crying beside his bed. His eyes shone and his face lit up. He was staring at something very pleasing and he wanted to tell the others what it was. He grew excited; he half-rose in the bed. Finally he grew taut, alive with enthusiasm.

"Look, Dad!" he cried pointing. "Look! Can't you see the wonderful . . . beautiful . . ." He stretched out his arms, reaching at what he saw.

No one ever knew what Dominic saw in his last ecstasy on earth, nor who it was that came to lead his soul to God. His arms dropped lifeless onto the bed and he fell back gently on the pillows. Dominic was dead.

The news reached Don Bosco the following day in a letter written by the boy's father.

"With tears in my eyes, I write you, Reverend Father," it said, "to tell you of the sad news. My dear little son, Dominic, your pupil, like a baby, like another St. Aloysius, gave his soul to God the evening of March 9 [1857], it being understood that he first received the Sacraments and the Papal Blessing."

The news shocked the Oratory into silence.

From the first announcement of his death, some of the boys began to pray not *for* but *to* him.

"The word of Dominic's death," wrote Don Bosco, "was received with consternation by his companions. Some felt they had lost in him a friend, a counselor; others, a model of a Catholic boy. A few did gather together to pray for the repose of his soul, but the majority declared that he was a saint and had already gone to heaven. They began to recommend themselves to him. Several of them set out on an excited search for objects in the Oratory that had once belonged to him." They already considered those objects as the relics of a saint.

On March 11, his remains were brought out for burial. A large crowd for such a small community gathered around the coffin that was laid in a poor grave in the little walled cemetery of Mondonio. Father Pastrone, later Pastor of Mondonio, remembered afterward that those who visited the grave uncovered their heads and knelt down to kiss the earth that lay on God's teenager.

There was no photograph of Dominic at the Oratory, for photography was not yet in common use. Hence, Don Bosco sought some other means of preserving Dominic's likeness to present him to his boys for study and imitation.

Calling in Tomatis, who was attending art courses at the Royal University of Turin, he asked him to reproduce a likeness of Dominic from memory. Although the finished product bears out the truth of the criticism that Tomatis must have been a mere beginner, nevertheless he at least preserved the principal characteristics of his friend.

Next appeared, in 1900, a picture made by another

artist who specialized in touching up photographic portraits. He touched up Dominic's features and made a new boy of him, a soulful, sad-eyed, irresolute creature, completely lacking character and determination. Because of the demand for pictures of Dominic Savio, however, this portrait, unfortunately, had a world-wide distribution.

Finally in 1941, M. Caffaro-Rorè, an artist of repute, undertook the task of bringing Dominic back to life. Using Tomatis' original effort as his guide, and all the documentary information he could gather, he gave us the picture of Dominic Savio that we have today. This was accepted by those who followed the question of the boy's appearance with close interest, as the nearest resemblance so far obtained.

Dominic was not heavily built, but rather graceful, and of medium height. Compared to the other boys, he was somewhat pale. His eyes were light blue, and they immediately attracted attention. His pale skin and blue eyes gave him a lighter complexion than is usually considered Italian, although in northern Italy this fair type is not by any means uncommon. His mouth was small and well-formed, and usually smiling, and this gave him a cheerful and lively look. It had also a determined set that indicated fixity of purpose. His hair was combed simply, for Dominic followed the spirit of the Oratory and avoided affectation.

This general picture lives up faithfully to what Dominic is known to have been — a pleasant-featured boy, blessed with a serene though sensitive disposition.

CHAPTER 18

THE SECRET LISTS

ABOUT a month after Dominic's death Charles Savio lay in bed one night unable to go to sleep. The memory of his son, for some reason or other, was particularly vivid to him that night. As he stared at the gray ceiling, he gradually grew aware of something odd. The ceiling above him began to glow, dimly at first, and then brightly. Finally it became a circle of light and in the center of the light appeared Dominic, radiant and smiling.

"Dominic! Dominic!" cried Charles. "Where are you? Where are you? Are you in heaven yet?"

"Yes, Dad, I am in heaven."

"Oh! If God has been so good to you, son, pray for your brothers and sisters that they may go to heaven, too!"

"All right, Dad. I'll pray for them."

"And pray for your mother and me that we may save our souls!"

"All right, Dad, I will."

The vision disappeared; the light grew dim, and the ceiling returned to its former dull gray.

Dominic's father, who in his old age came to live at the Oratory, was examined and re-examined on this apparition by Don Bosco. He was examined by others besides Don Bosco, but the good man simply repeated the same story over and over. To his knowledge he was not sleeping at the time, nor could he fall asleep for a long while afterward. Neither before then nor since, he said, awake or asleep, not even when he wanted to, had he been able to experience anything similar.

Later, on December 6, 1876, Don Bosco felt more inclined to believe the boy's father. He had a vision which the Holy Father made him put in writing. It was exceptionally long, and in substance it ran thus:

"I was standing on the raised edge of a wide plain," he wrote, "that stretched out far before me. From a distance a long, long line of people came walking slowly in my direction. When they came nearer I saw that they were all boys. Dominic, dressed in a shining white, bejeweled garment with a red cincture about his waist, was at their head.

"I understood then that the white splendor and jeweled beauty of his gown was symbolic of his clean heart. The red cincture, the color of blood, was the symbol of the great sacrifices he had made for purity. It showed me that to keep himself pure in the sight of God, he had been ready, if circumstances had ever called for it, to suffer martyrdom.

"He offered me a bouquet of roses, violets, sunflowers, gentians, some ears of wheat, lilies, and evergreens.

" 'What do these flowers mean?' I asked.

" 'They represent the virtues we must practice to please God,' Dominic explained.

" 'What are they, Dominic?'

" 'Roses for charity, violets for humility, sunflowers for obedience, gentians for penance, ears of wheat for frequent Holy Communion, lilies for purity. The evergreens mean that these virtues should last forever. They represent perseverance.'

" 'Tell me, Dominic,' I said, 'you have always practiced these virtues. What gave you the greatest consolation at the hour of death — purity?'

" 'Not that alone.'

" 'A good conscience?'

" 'That's a good thing, but it was not the greatest.'

" 'Hope of glory in heaven?'

" 'Not even that, Don Bosco.'

" 'What then? Having stored up plenty of merit?'

" 'No.'

" 'What, please?' I asked, embarrassed and confused.

" 'It was this: the assistance at death of the Mother of God. Tell that to the boys, Father. Tell them never to forget to pray to her all the days of their lives.' "

Don Bosco tried to get Dominic to tell him something of the happiness the saints enjoy. Dominic spoke of a beautiful light which, he said, Don Bosco now saw only dimly in the vision. Human nature could not stand to look at it directly.

"Can't you describe better what you enjoy in heaven?" Don Bosco asked.

"It's impossible to describe," Dominic said. "The only

thing I can tell you is this: We enjoy God."

Dominic then revealed clearly and precisely what the future held for the saint. Don Bosco, when he awoke, wrote down the predictions for he wanted to check them later with the actual events.

Here are the predictions with a brief explanation of each one's fulfillment:

Six boys and two clerics would die on given dates.

The six boys and two clerics died on the dates foretold. The registers of the Oratory state that two clerics and six boys in rhetoric class died in 1877. One of the clerics died December 31, 1877, in the last minute of the time limit set in the dream!

There was someone else besides Don Bosco interested in those particulars. Captain Piccono was in charge of the police precinct in which the Oratory was located. He came to hear of the prophecy and decided to do a little investigation on his own. He conscientiously followed each case through and checked each death against the date foretold.

When the eighth death occurred on its appointed day, Captain Piccono suddenly gave up his police career, joined the Salesians, and left for the missions in South America.

The name of the Salesians would expand quickly to the four quarters of the globe.

Don Bosco published his periodical, the *Salesian Bulletin,* in August, 1877. Translated into thirteen different languages, it quickly spread the name of the Salesians throughout the world. It is now printed in 22 different languages and is distributed in about 40 nations.

The next years of Don Bosco's life would be troubled ones.

Those acquainted with the saint's life know that, despite the astonishing success of his work, these were 12 years of almost constant persecution.

Most important of all the prophecies were the ones concerning the Holy Father, Pope Pius IX. Dominic had mentioned the Holy Father in the prophecy called "The Vision of England." Now he told Don Bosco that *the Holy Father had very little time left to suffer for the Church.*

Pope Pius had already suffered much for the Church. Toward the end of his reign matters had reached such a pitch that on September 20, 1870, General Bixio, one of Garibaldi's generals, was stopped from firing a cannon at St. Peter's dome by the threat of another officer that he would run his sword through Bixio's heart if he dared to fire that shot. It was then that the students of the American College in Rome offered to take up arms to defend the person of the Holy Father with their lives.

"The end of the Papacy is in sight!" sang the false prophets once again.

It happened as Dominic had foretold. Pope Pius IX, after a long and vexed reign of 32 years — the longest in the history of the popes — during which he was driven from the Vatican and expelled to Gaeta, died in Rome, February 7, 1878, a year and two months after Dominic's prophecy.

In the vision Don Bosco continued to ask Dominic questions.

"Are all my boys saved, Dominic?"

"The boys whom God has given you can be divided into three classes. You see these three sheets of paper?"

He handed Don Bosco three folded sheets of paper. On the first one were written the words: *not wounded.* It contained the names of those whom the Devil had never been able to lead astray. They had still preserved their purity of heart. There were a great many and he did not know them all. The ones he did not know were later to be boys in his schools. They walked noble, erect, and unafraid of the temptations the devils cast before them.

On a second sheet Don Bosco read the word: *wounded.* These were the names of those who had once fallen victims to temptation. Later, however, they had regained the grace of God. As in all three instances, he saw each boy before him as he read his name. This second list was the longest.

Those who are fixed in their evil ways was written on the third sheet. It was a list of those now living in mortal sin.

Impatient to know their names, Don Bosco stretched out his hand for the paper. Dominic stopped him.

"No. No. Wait a moment," he said. "When you unfold this there will rise from it a stench that will sicken you. Take it and use it for the good of your boys."

When he had finished, he drew back as if he wanted to escape. Don Bosco unfolded the sheet and at first saw nothing on it. Then he saw one by one the boys whose names were on the list, as if they were standing right before him. He recognized most of them, and many of them had the reputation of being good boys.

When he unfolded the paper it gave off such an abomi-

nable stench he thought it would actually kill him! The
sky grew clouded, the vision disappeared, and Don Bosco
heard a great clap of thunder. . . .

"When I awoke," Don Bosco wrote, "I was trembling
and the foul smell of the paper had penetrated the walls
and still clung to my clothes. For a long time afterward,
I could still smell that stench and even now the memory
of it makes me sick.

"I questioned one boy after another to check what I
had seen in the dream, and I found out to my sorrow
that the dream was true."

In letting Dominic leave the Oratory, God had His own
ends in view. The cemetery of St. Peter-in-Chains, where
all those who died at the Oratory were buried, was closed
some years later. The remains of the dead were removed
and indiscriminately buried in the new municipal burial
ground. Mama Margaret's remains, for instance, could
not be found again when, years afterward, it was decided
to re-inter them in a more suitable resting place. Had
Dominic died at the Oratory, he, too, would have been
buried in the cemetery of St. Peter-in-Chains and his
remains would have been lost forever.

The first pilgrimage to his grave at Mondonio was
organized on March 11, 1857, and became an annual
event. It was a local affair at first, conducted chiefly by
those who had known Dominic personally. They went to
pray at the grave that was always trimmed and cared
for by his father.

In 1859, a merchant from Genoa received a great favor
through Dominic's intercession. Out of gratitude he

ordered a more imposing headstone for the grave. News
of the favor and the headstone spread and gave further
impetus to the pilgrimages.

From that time on, devotion to Dominic increased so
much that the burial place was changed three times and
the coffin replaced once. Pilgrimages multiplied in number and size. Pilgrims even came from foreign countries.

Finally it was decided to have the remains removed to
the great church of Mary Help of Christians in Turin.
There they would lie beside those of Dominic's guide
and friend, Don Bosco.

Those responsible for the decision, however, reckoned
without the people of Mondonio. When the people of
Mondonio got wind of what was afoot, they set a guard
around the cemetery. No one was going to take "little
Savio" away from them, if they could help it. They loved
him too much for that. In the end their angry opposition
caused the plan to be dropped, at least for the time being,
and the important people who came to take away "little
Savio" had to leave without him.

After a great deal of further negotiation the matter was
reopened. This time the strictest possible secrecy was
observed. On the night of October 27, 1914, Dominic's
remains were removed in silence and under cover of dark-
ness, hurriedly brought to a waiting car, and driven off at
high speed in the direction of Turin. They were then laid
in their permanent resting place beside Don Bosco, in the
Basilica of Mary Help of Christians in that city.

CHAPTER 19

SIGNS AND WONDERS

TEENAGERS were the first ones to pray to Dominic, asking for his intercession. For the most part they were suffering from that ailment to which teenagers are often prone — toothache in varying degrees of intensity. Dominic began these cures on April 4, 1858, and they continued until they became no longer news. As the faith of Dominic's friends grew with an increase of evidence to support it, the cures became more impressive. To list all the cures made in those years is impossible, of course, although the records of them are preserved in Turin.

One of the early outstanding proofs of Dominic's intercession was the cure of Louis Castellano, a cleric studying with Don Bosco. He was stricken with an incurable disease and after having been examined by several doctors, was given up as hopeless.

"Two things are certain to happen soon," said Don Bosco. "Sicily will fall (to Garibaldi), and Castellano will go to heaven."

The days grew into weeks, the fall of Sicily became imminent, and Castellano asked Don Bosco to hear his last confession. After confession, however, the saint suddenly decided that he needed Castellano too much to let him go so easily. He appealed, therefore, to Dominic.

"If Dominic cures him now, it will be certain proof of his sanctity," he declared publicly, as if challenging the boy to do his best. That evening, to everyone's astonishment, Castellano rose up cured.

Some months after Castellano's recovery, Don Bosco returned from one of his begging expeditions in the city. He was met by his lieutenant, Father Alasonatti.

"Don Bosco," said the latter, excitedly, "if you want to see him before he dies, you'd better hurry."

"See who before he dies?"

"Young Davico. He had a terrible seizure in the stomach an hour or so ago. They've given him up."

"Ah, no," said Don Bosco smiling. "If Davico thinks he can go off like that without permission, he's much mistaken. I haven't signed his passport."

The saint reached the sickroom, and the crowd of boys separated to allow him near the bedside. He nodded to the doctor who stood looking gravely at the dying boy's contorted face. He bent over the boy, whispered into his ear, and invited the group to pray with him to Dominic Savio. When the prayers were ended, Don Bosco raised his hand to bless the dying boy.

Suddenly Davico shook himself. He sat upright in bed.

"I'm cured," he said abruptly.

Such a commotion in the room followed that nobody knew exactly what to do. Even Davico himself was at a loss, so unexpected was the cure.

"What do I do now?" he asked helplessly, appealing to the others.

"What you do now," said Don Bosco, taking command, "is get out of that bed and come down to supper with me. No, no . . . let him alone!" This was said to Father Alasonatti. More confused perhaps than any of the boys, he was nervously trying to help Davico dress.

"No," insisted Don Bosco. "If he wants to be cured, he's got to get up by himself."

Murmurs of warning rose against such haste. He might strain himself again; he might catch pneumonia after all that perspiration; he might . . .

"Don't worry," said Don Bosco a little impatiently. Then he turned to the boy. "Get up, Davico," he said. "Dominic Savio doesn't do things by halves. Come on, get up! You're going to have supper with me."

A perfectly recovered and exceedingly happy young Davico sat at Don Bosco's right that evening during supper.

Ever since then, Dominic kept on obtaining cures and favors, ordinary, extraordinary, and miraculous. Of the last kind, the two which follow were chosen by the Postulators of the Cause to fulfill the requirements for Beatification. Providentially, the miracles were granted to a boy and a girl, both teenagers.

Albano Sabatino was suddenly stricken at his home in Siano, Salerno, on March 27, 1927. Dr. Palmieri was called in, and found that Albano had an abdominal infection.

Two weeks after the first attack, Albano lost consciousness and entered into his agony. The doctor declared the boy could not be expected to live through the night. In the face of such certainty, he prepared the death certificate. This was to be given to the family the following morning as soon as the death was announced. A second doctor, called in by the parents as a last desperate gesture, found no reason to change the verdict of the first.

The next morning Dr. Palmieri returned. He was met by the parents. From the looks of them, they had evidently lost their reason in their sorrow. They were cheerfully discussing where they would send their son for a vacation.

When he saw the boy who, only the day before, had been dying, Dr. Palmieri's eyes nearly popped out of his head. Albano was sitting up in bed, laughing with the rest of the family, and telling them what he planned to do when the doctor let him get out of bed. Mystified but skeptical, Dr. Palmieri made a prolonged and detailed examination of his patient. When he had finished, he was forced to admit that the patient, in some way unknown to medical science, had been completely restored.

Albano's mother confessed that when she heard that her son was going to die, she had placed a picture of Dominic on the bedside table. Encouraged by the neighbors, she had also slipped a little card with a piece of Dominic's garment attached under the sick boy's pillow. From that moment the cure had begun.

Years later, in 1931 and 1933, as a necessary step toward the Cause of Beatification, a panel of experts was brought together to confirm the cure. They examined Albano and found absolutely no trace of his former complaint.

The second miracle of the Beatification took place in Barcelona, Spain. On March 1, 1936, while playing in the Oratory of the Salesian Sisters in Via Sepulveda, Consuela Adelantado, a schoolgirl, fell on her left elbow and felt a sudden stab of pain run through it. Consuela had an aunt who thought she could fix the elbow. The result was that a few days later, they had to bring the girl to Dr. Pamarola. He X-rayed the patient and found a double fracture of the arm with dislocation of bone splinters.

On the night of March 22, Consuela had a dream in which she saw a "priest" who told her to make a novena to Dominic Savio. He assured her that she would be cured by the following Friday and able to play the piano again. Shown photographs of several priests and dignitaries, Consuela had no difficulty in pointing out the one who had spoken to her about Dominic: Cardinal Cagliero.

Despite the skepticism of her family, who were not overly religious, Consuela began the novena in good faith on Friday, March 23.

All during the following Friday night she and her infirmarian did what they could to hasten the miracle. At one, two, three o'clock in the morning they were still trying. The only result of their labors was a red and dangerously swollen arm, and great pain. At four o'clock, in tears, Consuela pleaded with Dominic to do what the Cardinal said he would do. . . . Then a great weight seemed to fall from her arm, and she raised it as if nothing had ever happened to it!

She turned on the light and examined her arm: no wound, no swelling, no sign or feeling of anything wrong. Delighted, she kept the arm in motion until six thirty when she went to Mass. Then she telephoned the news that she was cured to the Sisters at the school. She recommenced her piano practice that same day.

Comparing X-ray photographs of the arm before and almost immediately afterward, the doctors had to admit and place on record "an instantaneous, perfect, and complete cure, in contrast to all natural laws."

Chapter 20

THE ROYAL SEAL

THE vicars of Christ always had a high regard for Dominic Savio. Pope Pius IX, the pope in Dominic's prophecy, did not have time to know him. But all the popes who succeeded him have held Dominic up as a model for the young.

St. Pius X said of Dominic to Cardinal Salotti: "He is the true model for the youth of our times. Anything you have so far said of him is too little. Do not waste time but push the Cause forward as fast as you can. When you finish his biography, I want you to bring me a copy. I shall read it willingly."

Pope Benedict XV said: "The 'Life of Dominic Savio' [by Cardinal Salotti] will prove more acceptable than that of St. Aloysius Gonzaga. This age no longer pictures to itself the saints as being so rigorous and penitential. The young will take to Dominic Savio because they can see in him one who was exactly like themselves." Pope Benedict XV used to recall with pleasure how, as a child, he had read the little "Life" of Dominic to his younger brothers in the presence of his mother. She had made up her mind, he said, to model her children after Dominic Savio. He also attributed his vocation to the reading of this book.

Pope Pius XI: "When we consider the conditions in which young people of the whole world find themselves today, the dangers and evil arts that threaten their Purity; the education to violence, to respect for nothing and nobody, we have every reason to thank God for having raised in our midst this edifying figure. At fifteen years of age, he was a true perfection of Christian life, with all those characteristics we need to be able to present him to the young people of our time. Oh, how much need there is to raise the banner of this splendor, this candor in the ranks of youth today! We have in Dominic Savio a providential gift of our own time."

Pope Pius XII: "Dominic Savio is the youngest Confessor of the Church, and a timely model for the youth of Catholic Action throughout the world."

Before the Church could canonize Dominic two more miracles had to be obtained through his intercession. Shortly after his beatification the following two miracles took place and were proposed:

In February, 1950, Mary Procelli Gianfrada of Maglie, Italy, felt unwell and her doctor, unable to find out what was wrong, ordered her to bed for a complete rest. A month later, March 23, together with other doctors, he re-examined her and found that she had acute internal hemorrhage and needed urgent attention.

The patient, meanwhile, grew so weak that her pulse

almost stopped and the doctor advised an immediate operation.

The relatives were so sure that the patient had only a few more moments to live they decided against the operation. They called in the priest instead.

The doctor had by chance been reading a life of Dominic Savio and he suggested that they pray to him for the sick woman. Since it was their only hope, they did so.

That night the patient began to improve so rapidly that the next morning she was declared to be out of danger. A well-known surgeon, however, recommended that she be brought to the hospital to have the residue of the blood in the intestines removed. But even this was found unnecessary because the patient's organs had been completely restored.

Mrs. Antoinette Nicelli Miglietta in September, 1949, felt a pain in her right jaw that spread to her head. After ten days of medical care it went away but came back again, this time accompanied by an unpleasant odor. She went to see a specialist but nothing he suggested did any good. Her temperature rose, her breathing became difficult, and she lost weight and strength alarmingly.

In March, 1950, she agreed to an operation. While she was waiting for the operation, her husband, to take her mind off the pain, opened up a newspaper in front of her. Glancing through it she came upon the picture of Dominic Savio. She began to say a few prayers for his canonization and fell into a deep sleep, the first sleep she had had in twenty-four days.

The following morning she woke up at dawn. She felt herself suffocating and sat up in bed unable to breathe because of an obstruction in her nose and throat. She coughed and the obstruction came out — a lump of chalk-like substance. She knew then that she was cured and fell asleep again.

Later she rose, had something to eat, and picked up the newspaper to find out if there was anything new in it about Dominic Savio. Here she read that he had died on the morning of March 9. She glanced up at the calendar on the wall: it was March 9.

The doctor stated after examination that there was no need of the operation, and at the end of a series of visits declared that his patient had received a "first class grace."

Both these miracles were approved by the Church and on June 12, 1954, Dominic Savio was canonized by Pope Pius XII.

In the long history of the Church Dominic is the first schoolboy not a martyr to be canonized. He is also the first saint in long pants. All the saints who went before him wore every other conceivable kind of clothing, but Dominic is the first saint in modern dress. Besides that, he is the first saint whose statue was already in St. Peter's even before he was canonized. In one of the niches reserved for the founders of religious orders stands the statue of St. John Bosco, eighteen feet high, with two boys by his side. One is a little South American Indian, Namuncurà, the Prince of the Andes; the other, with Don Bosco's hand resting lightly on his shoulder, is Dominic Savio.

So ends the story of the teenager who, in the words of the saint canonized two weeks before him, St. Pope Pius X, "is the true model for the youth of our own times."